D1709440

MODERN WORLD NATIONS

AFGHANISTAN
ARGENTINA
AUSTRALIA
AUSTRIA
BAHRAIN
BANGLADESH
BELGIUM
BERMUDA
BOLIVIA
BOSNIA AND
  HERZEGOVINA
BRAZIL
CANADA
CHILE
CHINA
COLOMBIA
COSTA RICA
CROATIA
CUBA
DEMOCRATIC REPUBLIC
  OF THE CONGO
THE DOMINICAN
  REPUBLIC
EGYPT
ENGLAND
ETHIOPIA
FINLAND
FRANCE

REPUBLIC OF GEORGIA
GERMANY
GHANA
GREECE
GUATEMALA
HAITI
HONDURAS
ICELAND
INDIA
INDONESIA
IRAN
IRAQ
IRELAND
ISRAEL
ITALY
JAMAICA
JAPAN
KAZAKHSTAN
KENYA
KUWAIT
MEXICO
NEPAL
THE NETHERLANDS
NEW ZEALAND
NICARAGUA
NIGERIA
NORTH KOREA

NORWAY
PAKISTAN
PANAMA
PERU
THE PHILIPPINES
POLAND
PORTUGAL
PUERTO RICO
RUSSIA
RWANDA
SAUDI ARABIA
SCOTLAND
SENEGAL
SOUTH AFRICA
SOUTH KOREA
SPAIN
SUDAN
SWEDEN
SYRIA
TAIWAN
THAILAND
TURKEY
UKRAINE
THE UNITED STATES
UZBEKISTAN
VENEZUELA
VIETNAM

Haiti

Charles F. Gritzner
South Dakota State University

CHELSEA HOUSE
An Infobase Learning Company

Frontispiece: Flag of Haiti

Cover: Terracing on small farm, Godet, Haiti.

Haiti

Chelsea House
An imprint of Infobase Learning
132 West 31st Street
New York NY 10001

Library of Congress Cataloging-in-Publication Data
Gritzner, Charles F.
  Haiti / Charles F. Gritzner.
    p. cm. — (Modern world nations)
  Includes bibliographical references and index.
  ISBN 978-1-60413-940-2 (hardcover)
  1. Haiti—Juvenile literature. I. Title. II. Series.

  F1915.2.G75 2011
  972.94—dc22
                          2010046923

Chelsea House books are available at special discounts when purchased in bulk
quantities for businesses, associations, institutions, or sales promotions. Please call
our Special Sales Department in New York at (212) 967-8800 or (800) 322-8755.

You can find Chelsea House on the World Wide Web at
http://www.chelseahouse.com

Text design by Takeshi Takahashi
Cover design by Alicia Post
Composition by EJB Publishing Services
Cover printed by Yurchak Printing, Landisville, Penn.
Book printed and bound by Yurchak Printing, Landisville, Penn.
Date printed: April 2011
Printed in the United States of America

10 9 8 7 6 5 4 3 2 1

This book is printed on acid-free paper.

All links and Web addresses were checked and verified to be correct at the time of
publication. Because of the dynamic nature of the Web, some addresses and links
may have changed since publication and may no longer be valid.

Table of Contents

Haiti

Introduction

Haitians have an old Creole proverb: *Deye mon, gen mon,* meaning "beyond the mountains, more mountains." Citizens of few countries in the world, and certainly none in the Western Hemisphere, have had more "mountains" to climb than have the Haitians. Some of these hardships have been cruelly imposed by natural forces such as killer hurricanes and earthquakes. Sadly, many other obstacles that appear insurmountable are self-inflicted. Hopelessly ineffective and corrupt government leaders, for example, are a primary cause of the country's chronic grinding poverty. Poverty, in turn, is a primary factor in many of Haiti's seemingly endless list of other problems. Through time, Haitians have learned to cope. They have bravely faced their mountain barriers and done the best they can to surmount them despite limited resources.

This is a study of Haiti from a geographical perspective. Simply defined, geography is the study of places, people, and conditions, with emphasis on their location and its importance. Geographers attempt to better understand the world and its varied features and patterns. In their search for answers, they basically ask "What is where, why there, and why care?" with regard to anything and everything on Earth's surface. Here, the focus is on Haiti and its fascinating physical and human landscapes and conditions.

Tropical island countries usually evoke images of sun, surf, and sand, with palms swaying gently in the breeze, and happy, carefree people going about their tasks. Some of these stereotypical images do hold true for Haiti, a country that shares the Caribbean island of Hispaniola with the Dominican Republic. Through time, however, this French-speaking land has suffered from repeated natural- and human-caused hardships. Raging hurricanes are frequent visitors to Hispaniola and other Caribbean islands. Their howling winds and drenching rain can leave a wake of death and destruction. Earthquakes are also a constant threat to life, property, and infrastructure. In January 2010 a massive quake struck the country's heartland. Port-au-Prince, the capital and largest city, was left in ruins, as were several other urban centers in the affected area. As many as three hundred thousand people died, and up to 2 million Haitians were left homeless and destitute. Many of the country's people saw their livelihoods destroyed as jobs and businesses vanished into the debris. Much of Haiti's heritage—its historical buildings, art, and countless other treasures—was reduced to rubble. It was an environmental disaster and resulting human tragedy on a scale previously unmatched in the Americas.

Haiti is the third largest country in the Caribbean region; only Cuba and the Dominican Republic are larger. The nation occupies the western third of Hispaniola, the island it shares with the Dominican Republic. Most of Haiti's 1,324-mile (2,131-kilometer) boundary is coastline. Northward, it faces the Atlantic Ocean and at a distance, various scattered islands of the southern Bahamas. Its western and southern boundaries

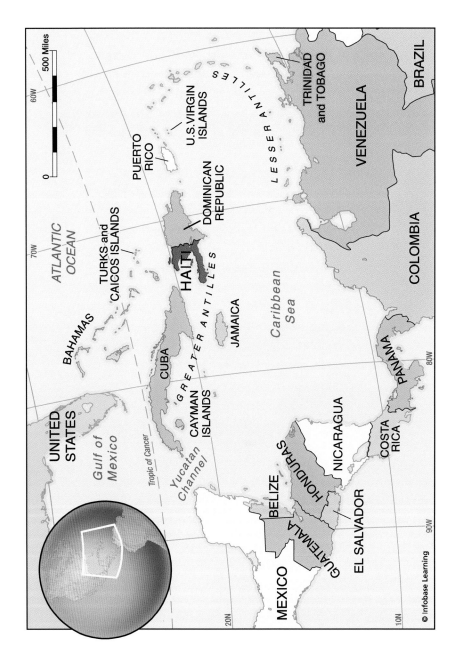

Haiti occupies the western third of Hispaniola, the Caribbean island it shares with the Dominican Republic.

face the warm tropical waters of the Caribbean Sea. Haiti also shares a 224-mile (360-km) land border with the Dominican Republic. Much of this boundary is formed by rivers, the Massacre in the north and Pedernales in the south.

Haiti, which became independent in 1804, is the second oldest country in the Americas (only the United States, which gained independence in 1776, is older) and is the world's oldest black-governed republic. Yet its history is one of tyrannical government, abject poverty, social turbulence, and massive human-caused environmental destruction.

Hispaniola is one of the Greater Antilles, a generally east-to-west trending archipelago (island chain) located between the Caribbean Sea and Atlantic Ocean. Its island neighbors are Cuba to the west, Jamaica to the southwest, and Puerto Rico to the east. The country lies roughly 600 miles (966 km) southeast of Miami, Florida. In territory, Haiti covers 10,714 square miles (27,749 square kilometers), an area slightly larger than Massachusetts, or roughly half the size of the Canadian province of Nova Scotia. Scattered about this relatively small territory, however, are an estimated nearly 9 to 10 million people. This is half again as many people as live in Massachusetts and ten times as many as reside in Nova Scotia. Haiti, more so than any other country in the Americas, suffers from having more people than its area, natural resources, economy, and infrastructure can adequately support. Not only is Haiti the poorest country in the Americas, it also ranks among the world's poorest and least stable lands.

While there are many positive things to be said for Haiti, the country suffers from many challenges to the quality of life of its citizens. The following list spotlights some of the first- and last-place rankings that Haiti holds within the Americas (all data are mid-2010 unless otherwise noted):

- Last in per capita income (about $300 following 2010 earthquake)

- Last in per capita gross domestic product ($1,300)
- Last in political stability (subjective assessment from various data)
- Last in life expectancy (60.8 years)
- Last in Human Development Index (HDI) (0.532; 149 among 182 countries ranked)
- Last in percentage of gross domestic product devoted to education (1.2%)
- Last in literacy (53%)
- Last in per capita oil consumption (1,431 barrels/day per 1,000 people)
- Last in per capita infrastructure development (subjective assessment from various data)
- First in deaths from a single natural disaster (estimated 230,000 from the 2010 earthquake)
- First in rate of natural population increase (2.1% per year)
- First in birthrate (31/1,000)
- First in death rate (10/1,000)
- First in infant mortality rate (60/1,000 live births)
- First in HIV/AIDS (2.2%)
- First in unemployment (estimated two-thirds of working-age population)
- First in Corruption Perception Index (1.8; 168 among 180 ranked countries)
- First in Failed States Index (11 among world countries)

- First country to elevate Voodoo (Vodou or Vaudou) to status of an official religion

- First in environmental degradation (subjective assessment based upon various data)

[**Note**: The list was compiled from various sources. Data vary greatly from source to source and year to year and should be used only to convey a general impression of conditions in Haiti.]

Travelers to Haiti who expect to find the country covered by a lush tropical rain forest are in for a disappointing surprise. Stereotypical wet, hot, lush conditions do occur, particularly in the far northeastern corner of the country. Nearly all of Haiti, however, falls within the Wet-Dry Tropical climate zone. During the high-sun (summer) season, conditions are hot, wet, and very humid; during the low-sun period (winter), very little rain falls and much of the land becomes parched. Small parts of the country receive only about 20 inches (51 centimeters) of rainfall annually. Such places are semiarid. Scrub vegetation dominates the landscape, and crops must be irrigated. Because much of Haiti is rugged mountainous terrain, temperatures vary with elevation. As is true throughout the tropics, temperatures in any particular location remain fairly constant throughout the year. In drier lowland areas, they can reach into the upper 90s (circa 36°C), yet, perhaps surprisingly, frost occurs at higher elevations. High temperatures are moderated somewhat by the northeast trade winds, which blow almost constantly.

Overall, nature has not been kind to Haiti. Because of the rugged terrain, little land is suitable for large-scale commercial agriculture. Further, it is both difficult and costly to build transportation linkages in mountainous areas. The broad-based practice of clearing steep slopes for fuel and farming has resulted in a monumental environmental disaster. As a result of deforestation, erosion is widespread. There are few mineral resources of commercial value, and Haiti has no fossil fuels. Because precipitation is extremely seasonal, river flow is

During Haiti's summers, conditions are hot, wet, and humid, and the landscape is lush. During the winter, however, the land becomes parched and needs to be irrigated.

unreliable. No streams are navigable by large vessels, and only 5 percent of the country's electricity is produced by hydroelectric facilities. As mentioned previously, environmental hazards pose an omnipresent threat to property and human life.

Haiti has a long and fascinating cultural history. Christopher Columbus landed on Hispaniola's north coast on December 6, 1492. The land he "discovered," however, had been home to Taino Indians for several millennia. The French, who colonized the region in the mid-seventeenth century, soon replaced the initial Spanish influence. For a time, Saint Domingue (as Haiti was then called) was the most prosperous of all French colonies. In fact, the colony earned the nickname "Pearl of the Caribbean." To work the plantations, French planters introduced black Africans as slave laborers. The horrible conditions led to slave revolts, which were ultimately successful: In 1804 Haiti became the world's first independent black republic.

Since gaining independence, however, Haiti has suffered almost constant political, economic, and social turbulence. Politically, the country has experienced few periods of stability. Economically, it remains the poorest country in the Western Hemisphere. When its government is unresponsive to people's needs and unable to ensure stability and provide adequate services, a country's economy is sure to fail. In Haiti the agony resulting from inept and inadequate institutions is compounded by nature's frequent wrath. It is little wonder that Haitian society is often strained to the limits of human endurance.

We will begin our journey through Haiti with a tour of its physical conditions. Because of the earthquake's importance, a separate chapter focuses on the January 12, 2010, quake and its aftermath. We will then glimpse back in time to learn about Haiti's history and how the past has played such an important role in molding the country's present conditions. People and culture (way of life), and government and economy, are discussed in detail. Finally, we will experience life in Haiti today and then gaze into a crystal ball to see what the future may hold for the country and its people. As you read on, keep a sharp eye out for clues to the meaning of *Deye mon, gen mon* (Beyond the mountains, more mountains).

2

Physical Geography

T his chapter is about the relationship between environment and culture, and about Haiti's physical geography—its land features, weather and climate, flora and fauna, and water features. You also will find out how these features and conditions have helped Haitians in some ways and hindered them in others.

ENVIRONMENT AND CULTURE

Cultural ecology is the study of how people culturally adapt to, use, and modify their natural environments. There are several ways to think about the environment and its importance. Some people, for example, believe that conditions of the natural environment direct people toward certain ways of living; nature essentially serves as a guiding hand. In this school of thought, "good" lands contribute to human well-being, whereas "bad" environments lead to poverty. This idea, they would argue, helps to explain Haiti. A rather poor environment, they suggest, has been a major contributor to the poverty of the country and its people. There are, however, some serious problems with this idea. Iceland, for example, is one of the world's coldest, most rugged, remote, and barren lands; yet the small country ranks at or near the top of any list of per capita wealth and human well-being.

Another view, quite the opposite of that just described, is that the environment simply "is." Those who take this position argue that the value of any natural setting is determined by people themselves. How do they use the land and resources? Do they have adequate technology and other capital resources needed to make the land productive? Are their political system and economy stable enough to encourage people to invest in the country? Mao Tse-tung, former leader of China, recognized the relationship between culture, land use, and human well-being. He suggested that there is no such thing as an unproductive area; rather, there are only unproductive people. His view certainly applies to Haiti. People who are poor, poorly educated, and poorly governed are unable to develop the potential their environment offers.

Let's use an artistic painting to illustrate the relationship between environment and culture. An artist has a surface—such as canvas, paper, glass, cement, wood, or cloth—on which a picture of some kind will be painted. In our analogy, this surface is the land itself. In no way does the surface determine what will be painted on it or, for that matter, the quality of the final work of art. Using brushes or other tools, the artist applies some medium, such as oil- or water-based paint, to create an image. Think of these items—the tool(s) and medium that are applied to create an image—as other environmental elements. They represent conditions of weather and climate, flora and fauna, soils and water features, and mineral resources. These may impose some limits, but such obstacles can be overcome. For example, an artist who

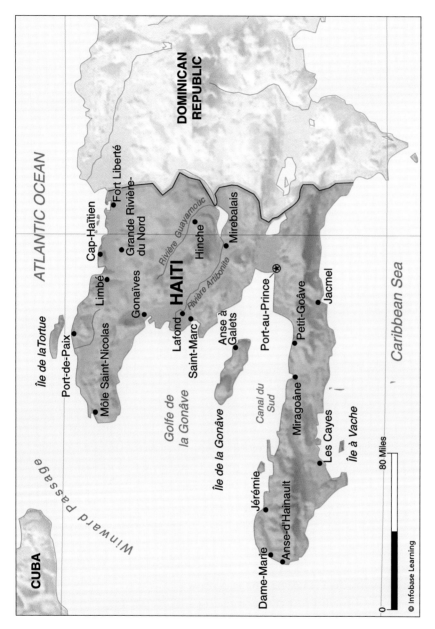

Haiti's rugged terrain creates challenges for farming, building infrastructure, and construction of settlements. Because it is more inhabitable, most Haitians live in the lowland plains, while the upland region is largely uninhabited.

needs a new brush or runs out of some color can purchase the needed item. Japan, one of the world's greatest industrial powers, offers an excellent example of overcoming obstacles. More than 95 percent of all natural resources and raw materials used in Japanese industry must be imported. Haiti, on the other hand, is far too poor to purchase all its needs from the global marketplace.

Finally, there is the finished work of art. It is entirely the result of the artist's selection of a medium with which to work and his or her resources, knowledge, skill, and ability to turn a mental image into a work of art. So it is with a people and the land they occupy. All humans, functioning as cultural groups, do three things as they interact with the natural environment: First, they must culturally adapt to the physical environment and the various conditions that it imposes. Second, they must identify and use (or misuse) a number of available natural elements. (Those that a culture uses become natural resources.) Finally, as they live on and work the land, they will change the environment in various ways, some good and others bad.

LAND FEATURES

Several conditions highlight Haiti's geological makeup. First, the island of Hispaniola is geologically part of an alpine (mountainous) arc that includes the mountains of far-eastern Cuba, and highlands of Jamaica and Puerto Rico. As a result, much of Haiti—about 80 percent of the country's land surface—features rugged terrain. There is relatively little land well suited to settlement, transportation linkages, or large-scale mechanized farming.

Second, Hispaniola sits atop several geologic faults, including the Enriquillo-Plaintain Garden Fault, the boundary between the very active North American and Caribbean tectonic plates. This condition has resulted in numerous and often severe earthquakes that seem to occur on a schedule of about one every 50 years.

Finally, Haiti resembles a horseshoe. Its open end faces westward toward Cuba, located about 60 miles (97 kilometers) to the northwest across the Windward Passage. The sides of the horseshoe represent Haiti's two long, rather narrow peninsulas that are formed by mountain crests that rise above the sea. They are separated by the Golfe de la Gonâve (Gulf of Gonâve), which occupies the empty center of the horseshoe. The horseshoe's arch is formed by a series of plateaus, mountains, and valleys. Haiti can be divided into three areas based upon terrain: the northern, central, and southern regions. There are also several nearby islands that belong to the country.

Three Regions

The northern region is dominated by the Massif du Nord. This mountain range extends westward into Haiti from the Dominican Republic and forms the northern peninsula. It is a relatively low range, with highest elevations reaching just over 3,600 feet (1,097 meters). Between the mountains and the sea, near the border with the Dominican Republic, is a small area of lowlands, the fertile Plaine du Nord (Northern Plain).

The central region includes several relatively low upland areas separated by narrow lowland plains. They include the Plateau Central (Central Plateau), which extends southward from the Massif du Nord. The plateau is divided into two sections by the fertile valley of the Guayamouc River. Southwest of the Central Plateau, the Montagnes Noires (Black Mountains) rise to elevations of just under 2,000 feet (610 m). To the south of this upland area is the 320-square-mile (829-square-kilometer) Plaine de l'Artibonite. This fertile lowland was formed by the Artibonite River, the longest stream on the island of Hispaniola. Two low mountain ranges, the Chaîne des Matheux and Montagnes du Trou d'Eau, form the southern margin of the central region.

The southern region includes the mountainous southern peninsula and Plaine du Cul-de-Sac. This area is Haiti's most densely populated region and also most rugged in terms of elevation. Here, in the eastern Massif de la Selle, Pic la Selle rises to an elevation of 8,793 feet (2,680 m), the highest point in the country. To the west, toward the end of the southern peninsula, Pic Macaya, in the Massif de la Hotte, rises to an elevation of 7,700 feet (2,347 m).

The Plaine du Cul-de-Sac, sandwiched between the central region and the southern peninsula, is a natural depression created by an active geologic fault. The valley, which extends into the Dominican Republic, reaches a maximum width of about 7.5 miles (12 km) and is only about 20 miles (32 km) long within Haiti. It is the most densely populated area of the country and includes the capital and largest city, the now devastated Port-au-Prince.

Islands

Haiti has a number of islands, several of which are inhabited. The largest is Ile de la Gonâve, located in the Golfe de la Gonâve northwest of Port-au-Prince. It was once a well-known base for pirates who preyed upon vessels as they sailed through the Windward Passage. Off the northwest coast lies Ile de la Tortue (Tortuga, or Turtle Island, so named because of its shape). It, too, was a major center for pirates who lay in wait for ships passing through the narrow waterway between Cuba and Hispaniola. Ile à Vache (Cow Island) is located in the Caribbean just off the southern shore of the southern peninsula.

Importance of Land Features

Rugged terrain covers about four-fifths of Haiti. As a result, farming, building linkages such as highways, and construction of settlements are difficult and costly. Widespread deforestation of mountain slopes and hillside farming have resulted in massive erosion. Most Haitians are crowded into the country's few small areas of lowland plains. Much of the upland region is quite isolated. It supports little economic activity, and population is sparse. Haiti lacks the capital resources, infra-structure, and stability needed to develop scenic highlands into tourist destinations. Overall, Haiti is more hindered than helped by the country's land features.

WEATHER AND CLIMATE

Of all natural elements, weather (day-to-day atmospheric conditions) and climate (long-term average conditions) are perhaps the most important. One need think only about the differences between equatorial and polar environments, or deserts and rain forests, to understand their significance. The flora, fauna, surface water, soils, and other features vary greatly from climate region to climate region. Of course, weather and climate are extremely important to humans and their activities as well. In the case of Haiti, it was the region's tropical conditions that played a major role in the country's culture and history.

Early Europeans settlers were drawn to the Caribbean, where the hot, wet climate favored the growing of tropical crops on large plantations. Midlatitude Europeans were, how-ever, poorly suited for strenuous physical labor in a tropical climate. Who then would work the fields? European planta-tion owners ultimately turned to Africans, who were brought as slaves to work the fields. Today more than 95 percent of all Haitians can trace their distant ancestry to Africa, and Haiti's culture is deeply etched with African traits.

Is that an example of environment determining culture? Not really. It was the culture itself, the European taste for sugar, for example, that created a perceived need for tropical sugar plantations. Plantation farming, itself, is an idea that grew out of Western European culture. The cultivation of sug-arcane appears to be a South Asian development, and so on. Haiti offers a marvelous example of cultural adaptation to the environment—people (acting as cultural agents) using a par-ticular natural setting for specific purposes. In this context, it is

interesting to note that when Africans began to govern themselves in Haiti, the plantation economy crumbled. Plantations
were a European idea, not African. Even today, Haiti is a very
minor producer of plantation crops.

Major Influences

Many factors influence the kind of weather and climate a location will experience. Five, in particular, stand out in regard to
tropical lands, including Haiti: latitude, elevation, proximity to
a large body of water, prevailing winds, and storms.

Latitude

Nearly all of Haiti falls between latitudes 18° and 20° north.
This places the country squarely at the northern edge of the
American tropics. People often think of all tropical places as
being hot and wet year-round, but this is not necessarily true.
Many definitions of *tropical* are based solely on temperature,
rather than on both temperature and moisture conditions. A
tropical location, then, is one in which the average temperature
of the coolest month is above 64.4°F (18°C) and frost occurs
only at high elevations. Because the sun is always high in the
daytime sky in tropical lands, average temperatures are quite
high throughout the year.

Elevation

Under normal conditions, temperatures drop with increased
elevation and altitude. (Elevation is distance above sea level of
a land-based location; altitude is distance above sea level at a
point within the atmosphere.) On average, temperature drops
about 3.5°F with every 1,000-foot (1.6°C per 305-m) increase
in elevation. If, for example, the temperature at Port-au-Prince,
located near sea level, is 80°F (26.6°C), one might expect that
atop 8,793-foot (2,680-m) Pic la Selle the temperature would
be about 31°F degrees cooler, or a pleasant 49°F (9.4°C). If, on
the other hand, the sea-level temperature drops to the mid-

60s, high elevations can experience frost. In a mountainous country such as Haiti, upland temperatures can be "springlike" throughout the year.

Proximity to a Large Body of Water

Have you ever noticed that when cold late-autumn temperatures arrive and the ground freezes, a lake remains ice free for some time? Or that in the spring, after the snow is gone and the ground has thawed, a body of water remains frozen for a while? This is because water heats and cools much slower than does land. Also, a body of water will not get as hot or cold as an adjacent land mass will. Therefore, land located near a large body of water will not experience high and low temperature extremes common to inland locations. Haiti, as a small island country, therefore benefits from the temperature-moderating effect of surrounding water.

Prevailing Winds

Most lands located between roughly the equator and latitude 30° degrees north experience northeast trade winds—winds that blow from the northeast most of the year. (Winds are named for the direction *from* which they blow.) These winds affect Haiti's climate in several ways. First, they tend to lower the heat index—the temperature that one actually feels on a hot day. (This is the same principle as people feeling cooler and more comfortable on a hot day when in front of a fan.) Many midlatitude vacationers take advantage of this condition. Even though tropical conditions prevail, the combined influences of the sea and cooling effect of the northeast trade winds make the islands a pleasant destination, even in the summer. As they cross the warm Atlantic, the trade winds also pick up moisture, which they release over land in the form of rain. Finally, the distribution of rainfall in Haiti is influenced by the combined influence of winds and mountain barriers.

Storms

The Caribbean (and many other tropical and subtropical locations) lies within the path of tropical storms. A tropical storm (also called tropical cyclone or tropical depression) has wind velocity between 39 and 73 miles (63 and 117 km) per hour. When wind speed is 74 miles (119 km) per hour or higher, the storm is classified as a hurricane. (Intense tropical storms in the Atlantic and Pacific coasts of the Americas are called hurricanes. They are called typhoons in the central and western Pacific Basin and cyclones in the Indian Ocean.) Such storms are frequent visitors to the Caribbean during the hurricane season, which officially lasts from June 1 to November 30.

Haiti has been struck by countless hurricanes, far too many to discuss individually. Here, the hurricane season of 2008 is used to illustrate the tremendous damage and incredible hardship these ferocious storms can inflict on Haiti. In that year, four major storms—Fay, Gustav, Hanna, and Ike—struck the country. Torrential rains fell, including on mountains stripped almost bare by widespread deforestation. With little vegetation to hold back the runoff, water gathered rapidly and cascaded down slopes, causing massive flooding in the valleys below. ReliefWeb.org gives the following toll inflicted by storms that struck Haiti in 2008:

- 793 deaths

- 310 people missing

- Nearly 600 people injured

- About 23,000 homes destroyed and another 85,000 damaged

- About 800,000 people affected

- 70 percent of the country's crops destroyed (eventually resulting in many more deaths from starvation)

- More than $1 billion in damage

Although the year 2008 was the most costly storm season in the country's history up to that time, many other years brought severe storms that resulted in widespread destruction and tragic loss of life. The following list includes only major storms of the twentieth century:

   1935—unnamed storm, killed more than 2,000 Haitians
   1954—Hazel, more than 1,000 deaths
   1963—Flora, estimated 8,000–8,500 lives lost
   1994—Gordon, more than 1,000 deaths
   1998—Georges, more than 400 deaths and more than 80
      percent of crops destroyed

Conditions

As a tropical country, Haiti's weather and climate can be described as hot, wet, humid—and monotonous. It has been said that "nighttime is the winter of the tropics." Diurnal (daily) temperature ranges, although not great, far exceed seasonal extremes. In Port-au-Prince, for example, the daily temperature range averages about 11°F (6°C), considerably greater than the annual range. There is very little change in daily conditions from season to season. Haiti, of course, is located at the far northern edge of the tropics. Therefore, it does experience slight seasonal variations of both temperature and rainfall. (See Figure 1.)

Temperature

If you want to avoid the hottest, most humid, sweltering season of the year, the best time to visit Haiti is during the Northern Hemisphere's low-sun (winter) season—November through March. Daytime temperatures at low elevations reach only into the 70s to 80s (20s to low 30s C) during this time of year. Summer conditions are somewhat warmer, with afternoon highs usually in the 80s to low 90s (25°–35°C). Temperatures are generally rather pleasant year-round because of the cooling effect of the trade winds. At night, depending upon the season, temperatures drop into the mid-60s and 70s (18°–27°C).

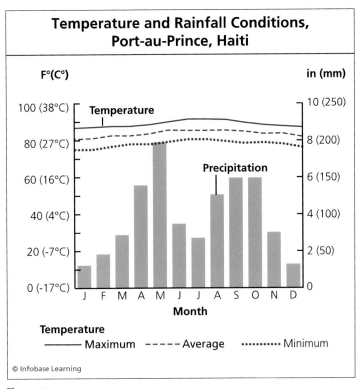

Temperature and Rainfall Conditions, Port-au-Prince, Haiti

F°(C°)

in (mm)

Temperature

Precipitation

Month

Temperature
——— Maximum - - - - Average ••••••••• Minimum

© Infobase Learning

Figure 1

Port-au-Prince has recorded temperature extremes of 100°F (37.7°C) and 61°F (16.1°C).

Elevation, of course, plays an important role in determining temperatures, with highland areas being considerably cooler and more pleasant. The importance of elevation is illustrated by temperatures in Port-au-Prince, located near sea level, and the town of Kenscoff, perched at about 4,700 feet (1,433 m) above sea level. The capital has an annual average of 79°F (26°C), whereas the highland village averages about 60°F (15.5°C).

Precipitation

The average annual rainfall for most of the country varies from about 50 to 80 inches (127 to 203 centimeters), but the distribution of precipitation is uneven both seasonally and by location. Port-au-Prince receives an average 53 inches (135 cm) of rainfall each year, about the same amount as the wettest U.S. state, Louisiana. The wet season begins in March and extends through October. During this soggy period, an average 6 to 10 inches (15 to 25 cm) of rain falls each month. Most of the rain falls as brief, though often torrential, thunderstorms from towering cumulonimbus clouds. During the dry season, which begins in November and lasts through February, only about 2 inches (5 cm) of rain falls each month.

Precipitation also is unevenly distributed throughout the country. Heaviest rainfall occurs on the northern and eastern mountain slopes that face the moisture-carrying northeast trade winds. As wind blows upslope, the air cools, moisture condenses, and rain falls on the windward slopes. On the lee-ward (downwind) southern and western slopes, conditions are drier. Wettest areas include the southern peninsula and northern plains and mountains. The driest parts of the country are in a belt that extends from the western part of the northern peninsula, southward to Port-au-Prince. In the far northwest, only about 20 inches (51 cm) of rain falls in some locations.

The frequent tropical storms that strike Haiti often result in torrential rainfall that surges down deforested mountain slopes and causes massive flooding. In 1963, Hurricane Flora dropped as much as 57 inches (145 cm) of rain over parts of the country. During the passage of several storms in 2008, much of Gona-ïves, Haiti's fourth largest city, was under more than 6 feet (2 m) of floodwater.

FLORA AND FAUNA

Haiti's original flora and fauna have been drastically changed by human activity. Cutting forests for fuel, clearing land for farming, and livestock grazing have all taken a huge toll on the country's plant and animal life. So drastic has the destruction of natural flora and fauna been that it is difficult to know what conditions were actually like before the arrival of humans. It is estimated that 98 percent of the original forest cover has been destroyed. Most of the loss has been for fuel used in cookstoves in energy-poor Haiti. Nearly all of the country's original native fauna is gone as well, replaced by domestic animals.

Some pines remain in higher mountainous regions, and cedars, mahogany, and oaks are found scattered about some protected valleys. There are an estimated five thousand plant species in the country, but few are of commercial value or of much use to Haiti's dirt-poor rural population. They include about six hundred species of ferns and three hundred different types of orchids. About one-third of the country's plant species are found only on the island of Hispaniola. Perhaps surprisingly, species of cacti can be found in drier parts of the country.

Most of Haiti's original wildlife is but a distant memory. Insects and birds abound, as do lizards and frogs. There are 15 different kinds of bats and 8 different kinds of rodents, some of which are considered to be a delicacy. The hutia, for example, was a staple of the original Amerindian (American Indian) inhabitants. Iguanas are common in some locations, as are crocodiles in some waters. The largest wild animal is the aquatic and odd-looking manatee, or sea cow, which is endangered.

One wild animal deserves special mention—the Hispaniolan solenodon, one of the world's strangest and rarest creatures. The solenodon is about the size of a large rat. Its body is stocky. As an insectivore, it has a long snout resembling that of an anteater and tapered claws designed to dig for insects. What makes the solenodon so unique, however, is that it is one of the world's few venomous mammals. Venom is injected from the animal's grooved teeth into its victim. Scientists believe that the shrewlike animal has existed for more than 75 million years. Today, however, it is endangered. Efforts are under way to protect the remaining small number of these rare creatures.

WATER FEATURES

Other than the surrounding waters of the Atlantic Ocean and Caribbean Sea, Haiti does not have any water features of major importance. There are many small streams that flow from the highlands. With Haiti's wet-and-dry seasonal rainfall, it is a case of "feast or famine" for the streams. Most, if not all, slow to a trickle or even dry up during the dry season. Then, during the wet season, they can swell to raging torrents and cause local flooding.

Haiti's largest river system is the 250-mile-long (402-km) Artibonite. It begins as the Lebón River in the Massif du Nord. The stream flows into the Dominican Republic and then returns to Haiti, where its name changes to Artibonite. As the river leaves the highlands, it flows through the Plaine de l'Artibonite where it leaves fertile alluvial (stream-deposited) soils. Finally, the river flows into the Golfe de la Gonâve. During the dry season, the stream is only several feet (approximately 1 m) deep and even dries up in some places.

Other major streams include Les Trois Rivières in the north, and the Guayamouc River, a tributary of the Artibonite. During the wet season, small boats can navigate the lower stretches of the larger rivers, but the streams are of little use for navigation or other economic activity other than local fishing. Haiti's only hydroelectric facility is the Peligre Dam, which forms Lake Peligre, located on the southern part of the Central Plateau.

Haiti also has several lakes. Ètang Saumâtre (also called Lake Azuei) is the country's largest body of water and the second largest lake in the entire Caribbean region. It is located on the Plaine du Cul-de-Sac along the border with the Dominican Republic in the southeastern part of the country. Because the lake occupies a basin of interior drainage (no water flows out of the basin), its water is salty. It is famous for the more than one hundred species of birds, including colorful flamingos, that spend at least part of the year there. Its deep blue waters also are home to the American crocodile. During recent years, the water level of Étang Saumâtre has risen, causing problems for people who live along its shore.

There are two other lakes of local importance: salty Trou Caïman is located near Étang Saumâtre in the semiarid Plaine du Cul-de-Sac east of Port-au-Prince; Lake Miragoâne is a large freshwater body located in the middle of the southern peninsula near the city of the same name.

ENVIRONMENTAL ISSUES

Haiti faces a number of environmental problems. Some, such as the devastation inflicted by earthquakes and hurricanes, can be anticipated, but not stopped. Others, such as deforestation and pollution, can be prevented or lessened in their impact. So can desertification, the creation of desertlike conditions through poor land-use practices. Poverty, pollution, and poor land-use practices go hand in hand. Only an affluent society can afford the luxury of a "clean" and sustainable environment. Poor people—and most Haitians certainly are poor—see the natural environment as a source of economic opportunity. To them, resources are there to be used. Trees, for example, are free fuel. More than 85 percent of all energy used in Haiti comes from charcoal, a fuel made from trees. As a result, Haitians have cut more than an estimated 98 percent of the country's original natural vegetation. Deforestation is so widespread and complete, in fact, that the boundary between Haiti and the Dominican Republic is one of the few in the world that is clearly visible from satellites.

Some areas of the country are being turned into a semidesert environment. Desertification is occurring as a result of land clearing, overgrazing, and farming marginal soils, particularly in Haiti's drier areas.

Pollution is widespread in nearly all heavily populated areas. The country and its citizens simply cannot afford adequate facilities for the sanitary disposal of garbage, sewage,

This satellite image of the border between Haiti and the Dominican Republic shows a clear line of deforestation. Haiti is depleting its forests in order to produce fuel.

and other waste. Much of the pollution, as you might expect, enters the domestic water supply. As a result of widespread consumption of contaminated water, Haiti has the highest death rate and infant mortality rate of any country in the Americas.

No natural event has had a greater effect on Haiti and its more than 9 million people than did the catastrophic earthquake that struck Port-au-Prince and adjacent communities in January 2010.

CHAPTER

3

The 2010 Earthquake

The afternoon of January 12, 2010, was a typical Thursday in bustling Port-au-Prince and neighboring communities. Little did residents know that they were soon to experience a shocking jolt, one that would catastrophically change their lives and country forever. At 4:53 P.M., the earth beneath their feet began to tremble and roar. A horrible disaster was striking the Western Hemisphere's poorest country. Measured at a magnitude of 7.0, the earthquake struck Haiti's capital and largest city and surrounding communities. The initial shock was followed by more than 50 others that measured 4.5 or higher.

WHAT CAUSED THE EARTHQUAKE?

Many Haitians have ideas of what caused the earthquake that might seem rather strange to readers. Some Christians are convinced that it was a sign or a warning of God's anger over various human sins.

Some Voodoo leaders similarly believe that it was caused by some message-bearing mystical force.

The answer, however, lies in the region's geology. Haiti, it is often said, is a "disaster waiting to happen." The island of Hispaniola and the country of Haiti are located in a very hazardous position. As a result, the country has a long history of earthquakes, many of which have resulted in extensive loss of life and destruction of property.

Hispaniola lies on top of two tectonic plates, the Caribbean and North American. The Caribbean plate is active, slipping eastward by about 0.79 inches (20 millimeters) a year. In Haiti, the strike-slip fault system branches into two separate fault zones. The Enriquillo-Plantain Garden Fault is in the south, beneath Port-au-Prince. In northern Haiti, the Septentrional-Oriental Fault also has caused numerous devastating earthquakes.

Most seismologists (scientists who study earthquakes) believe that it was the Enriquillo-Plantain Garden Fault that gave way to cause the January 12, 2010, rupture. In the area of the earthquake's epicenter (center point), the fault had been locked in place for about 250 years. The entire fault system, however, had continued to slip. When it finally ruptured, the land snapped like a rubber band. All along a 40-mile (64-kilometer) zone, the ground lurched about 6 feet (1.8 meters).

Some experts believe that the earthquake may actually have been caused by a previously undetected fault. If seismologists find this to be the case, Haiti's position is even more precarious than previously thought. To add to the uncertainty, earthquakes in this fault zone historically tend to occur in clusters. When one happens, it is soon followed by others.

THE EARTHQUAKE STRIKES

The earthquake could not have happened in a worse location. Some 3.5 million people were tightly clustered in the area

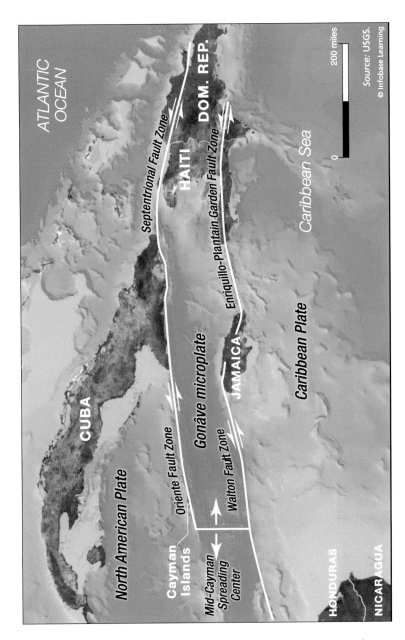

United States Geological Survey (USGS) map showing the location of
the Enriquillo-Plantain Garden Fault Zone.

directly affected. That is approximately 38 percent of Haiti's entire population. Its epicenter was located about 16 miles (26 km) west-southwest of Port-au-Prince. Slippage occurred rather close to the surface, at a depth of about 8 miles (13 km). So strong was the tremor that it was felt as far away as Puerto Rico, Jamaica, and even Venezuela. At least some of the earthquake's severe damage to Port-au-Prince and several other communities was the result of still another geologic condition. Much of the highly populated area is built upon loose sediments, rather than on hard rock. Unlike more stable hard rock, sediments shake like Jell-o when a quake strikes. This condition contributes to much greater structural damage.

Earthquakes usually are followed by aftershocks, and this event was no exception. Eight aftershocks struck within two hours of the main shock. During the 12 days following the main quake, a total of 52 aftershocks occurred. As you can imagine, these events, which measured 4.3 to 5.9, kept the Haitians and relief workers on constant edge.

THE TOLL

By the time the earth stopped shaking, much of southwestern Haiti, including Port-au-Prince and a number of other communities in the affected region, were reduced to rubble. The awesome toll of life and property taken by this earthquake will never be fully known, but it was staggering. In terms of the percentage of a country's population killed (estimated to be as high as 3 percent), it was one of the most horrendous events in history. The same holds true when the destruction's economic cost is measured against the country's gross domestic product (GDP). According to many estimates, the final cost will be a whopping $15 billion, more than double the country's 2010 estimated GDP.

Human Losses

Although estimates vary, the Haitian government placed the official death toll at 230,000. Another 300,000 people were injured, many of them severely. In the months following the earthquake, thousands of others died from their injuries, various infectious diseases, or starvation. Most experts agree that, at best, all fatality figures are estimates and that the true number of earthquake-related deaths will never be known. As measured by loss of life, it was the tenth most devastating natural disaster in world history. In terms of the number of fatalities, it ranks as the greatest natural disaster ever to strike the Americas.

Thousands of people were buried in the debris of poorly constructed buildings that collapsed under the shock. Morgues were overwhelmed with bodies. Tens of thousands of decomposing human corpses littered the streets, some lying in the sun for days. The stench of decaying bodies was sickening. On January 23, the Haitian government called off the search for survivors. Following the quake, about 135 people had been pulled from beneath the debris alive. Miraculously, one person was discovered on February 8, having survived for nearly one month in the rubble of a grocery store. Many, if not most, of the dead were buried in mass graves. Their bodies were transported by truck and unceremoniously dumped into 20-foot-deep (6-m-deep) trenches dug by earth movers and dirt-covered by bulldozers.

Most casualties were Haitian civilians, but many foreigners and Haitian public figures also lost their lives. Among the dead were tourists, aid workers, embassy staff members, and others in the country to help the Haitian people. The toll included nearly 90 United Nations (UN) workers, including the mission chief and his deputy. Some 200 people died in the collapse of the Montana, a hotel popular among foreign visitors. Well-known figures to die included the Catholic archbishop of Port-au-Prince; many popular artists, musicians, and sports figures (including 30 members of the country's football [soccer] team); one of the country's major opposition political leaders; and many Haitian government officials.

Structural Damage

It is often said that earthquakes don't kill people; bad buildings kill them. This certainly was the case in the Haitian disaster. Haiti's building codes are weak or nonexistent and where they do exist, enforcement is lax. Most construction is of very poor quality, as are the materials used in building. Many of the buildings in Port-au-Prince were constructed with handmade concrete blocks that weigh but a fraction of those made in the United States and Canada. They are poorly made, cheap, and easy to use. Such structures simply were unable to stand up to the force of the earthquake's harsh jolts.

The estimated 250,000 homes and 30,000 commercial buildings destroyed by the earthquake in Port-au-Prince represent a large portion of the city's built environment. Many government and other public structures also were lost. Government buildings destroyed include the National (presidential) Palace, the capitol building, the Palace of Justice (Supreme Court), the National Assembly (parliament building), and the Port-au-Prince City Hall. One of the city's most majestic buildings, the magnificent Port-au-Prince Cathedral, lay in ruins. The city's main prison also was destroyed, allowing some four thousand hardened criminals to escape.

An estimated half of the country's schools and at least three major universities were destroyed; so were most of the region's hospitals, museums, churches, art galleries (and many priceless artworks), and other public buildings. Many of the country's manufacturing and business facilities also were lost. These losses resulted in hundreds of thousands of people—an estimated 20 percent of the country's previously employed population—being left without jobs. In a land already suffering from staggering poverty and unemployment, the loss of jobs was tragic.

Equally hard hit was the infrastructure needed to respond to the disaster. All area hospitals were destroyed or severely damaged. The control tower and other structures at Toussaint

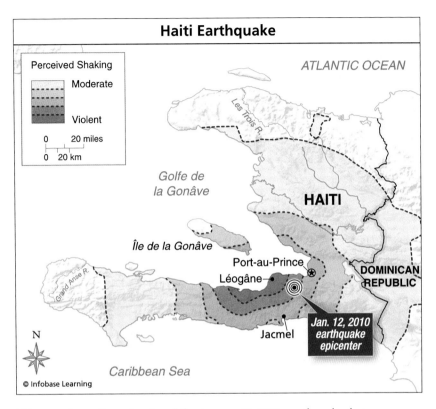

This map shows the epicenter of the January 12, 2010, earthquake that devastated Haiti.

Louverture International Airport were damaged. So was the city's seaport facility. Both were unable to receive aid shipments in the days immediately following the earthquake. Roads were choked with rubble, making surface transportation difficult to impossible within the city and elsewhere. The main highway between Port-au-Prince and Jacmel was impassable for 10 days following the quake. Communication networks were down. The public telephone system was shut down, and the area's two major cell phone providers were temporarily affected. Most of the radio stations were knocked off the air. Other municipalities in the affected area also suffered severe damage. In nearby

Léogâne and Jacmel, for example, up to 90 percent of all buildings collapsed.

Immediate Postquake Conditions

"Total chaos" best describes conditions in the areas affected by
the earthquake. Basically, more than 2 million people were milling about in search of food, water, and places to sleep. Even if
their houses survived, many Haitians were afraid to return home,
in fear that the structures might collapse from an aftershock.

The Haitian government was totally unprepared to take
charge and respond in a positive manner to such a huge disaster. There was total confusion over who—individuals, agencies,
governments—was in charge of the relief effort. In the absence
of strong organizational leadership from the Haitian government, many groups adopted a "Lone Ranger" approach. They
simply took command and acted without waiting for instruc-
tions. Several days passed before there was even a sign of organization in the relief effort. One of the first official delegations
of authority made by the Haitian government was to give the
United States control of Port-au-Prince airport operations.

All systems vital to the relief effort were damaged or
destroyed by the earthquake. Nearly all buildings were reduced
to rubble. Tens of thousands of bodies lay beneath the debris,
or on the sidewalks and streets. Thousands more were injured,
many seriously; yet hospitals were in ruins, many health-service
workers had been killed or injured, and essential medical supplies were unavailable. (According to estimates, perhaps thirty
thousand people died of injuries sustained in the quake simply
because they could not get medical attention.)

It was all but impossible to move about by land, water, or
air. Transportation facilities were destroyed, and the routes
were clogged with debris, making them impassable. Electrical
and most communications systems were inoperative. Food and
clean water were nowhere to be found. For days after the event,
no agency was in control. These were just some of the problems

faced by Haiti and its people in the days immediately following the earthquake.

Getting supplies into the country and distributed to those in need was a major priority. So was providing medical care for the injured; and getting food, water, adequate sanitation facilities, and shelter to those in need. As you can imagine, there were long delays responding to these needs. As a result, widespread anger led to looting and occasional violence. In some areas, conditions were so bad that relief workers simply stayed away. According to several reports, corrupt Haitian customs officials actually prevented relief vehicles from entering the country from the Dominican Republic until bribes were paid. Yet according to reports, in the days following the earthquake, there were many acts of human kindness and compassion. Thousands of people took to the streets in peaceful processions, singing, dancing, clapping, and praying.

THE INTERNATIONAL RESPONSE

The humanitarian response to the Haitian tragedy was swift and overwhelming. Within days, more than 60 countries had responded in some way. UN Secretary-General Ban Ki-moon announced that some $9.9 billion had been pledged over a period of three years to help rebuild the earthquake-ravaged country. He noted that the donations were "far beyond expectations."

The first country to respond was neighboring Dominican Republic, which sent emergency medical teams. They also contributed heavy-lifting equipment, food and water, and mobile kitchens and cooks able to produce 100,000 meals daily. Tiny Iceland was the first distant country to come to Haiti's aid. Within 24 hours of the disaster, the country's world-famous Icelandic Association for Search and Rescue (ICE-SAR) unit arrived to search the rubble for bodies.

The response from the United States and Canada was massive. Both countries provided highly skilled human resources, technical assistance, equipment, and huge financial support. In the United States, a number of entertainers joined together for a "Hope for Haiti Now" telethon that raised more than $57 million for relief. Participating stars included Beyoncé, Brad Pitt, Bruce Springsteen, George Clooney, Justin Timberlake, Kid Rock, Madonna, Shakira, and Sting. Haitian-born Wyclef Jean, a famous hip-hop artist, also performed.

Various international agencies, including the UN, the International Red Cross, and Doctors Without Borders responded. To coordinate long-term redevelopment efforts, a 26-member international Interim Haiti Reconstruction Commission was formed. Headed by former U.S. president Bill Clinton and Haitian prime minister Jean-Max Bellerive, it first met to begin work in June 2010.

The response was a heartwarming illustration of how the world—despite our many differences and conflicts—can pull together in a time of crisis.

STEPS TOWARD RECOVERY

Two months after the earthquake, Ben Fox and Jonathan Katz, Associated Press writers, described conditions in Port-au-Prince as follows:

> Trash and sewage are piling up at the squalid tent camps that hundreds of thousands have called home since Haiti's devastating earthquake—and with torrential rains expected [summer is the hurricane season] . . . authorities are not even close to providing the shelters they promised.
>
> Two months since the [the earthquake] . . . the government has yet to relocate a single person. . . . Aid groups say they're ready to build but don't have the land. Government officials insist they are making progress on finding sites. . . . But time is running out for 1,600,000 people living under tarps, tents or simply

bed sheets.... People in the crowded camps—mazes of rough shelters where the air is thick with flies, mosquitoes and the stench of overflowing pit latrines—say they can't wait much longer for better conditions.

Six months after the earthquake, little had changed. An estimated 98 percent of the rubble had not been removed. Most of Port-au-Prince remained impassable. Very little new housing had been built, and an estimated 1.3 million people still lived in the squalid camps. Summer rains had turned the camps into soggy, muddy, unbearable messes. Most camps lacked electricity and adequate sanitation facilities, including sewage disposal and clean water. Crime was widespread.

By the end of 2010, Haiti's nightmare continued, seemingly without end. A cholera epidemic broke out in mid-October. The deadly disease, spread mainly by drinking contaminated water, also had sickened an estimated 125,000 people by the end of the year. Well over one million people still lived in the flimsy tent settlements. They were extremely vulnerable when Hurricane Tomas struck the island in early November with torrential rains and high winds. Many people were afraid to leave the tent villages. Most had nowhere else to go. And nearly everyone was afraid to leave their personal belongings behind, unguarded. When the storm hit, tent villages were leveled. Floodwaters raged through the streets and rubble of Port-au-Prince and other communities. And mudslides, caused by super-saturated earth, killed at least seven people. Haitians wonder when, or even if, their horrible nightmare will end.

Most displaced people continue to live under desperate and squalid conditions. According to a UN report, more than one million people are still living in 1,300, mostly unmanaged, camps. Sexual and other types of violence are rampant, and gangs freely prey upon the hapless refugees.

Government plans for relocation progress at a snail's pace. One major problem is that few Haitians, perhaps only 15

A man walks in the rubble of the collapsed Port-au-Prince Cathedral after the 2010 earthquake. Thousands of buildings were destroyed by the earthquake, including several important government structures.

percent of them, actually hold title to the land on which they live. They are squatters. Much of the land is owned by wealthy Haitians whose ownership goes back many generations. Understandably, they do not want to part with their property and see it turned into resettlement villages. Often-heated negotiations between the government and landowners continued months after the quake. According to one government estimate, it will cost nearly $130 million to secure land and build relocation camps. The government, however, simply does not have the needed financial resources to do this. Rather, some people fear that it will seize private property on which to build the resettlement camps.

LESSONS FROM TWO TRAGEDIES

Valuable lessons can be learned from two earthquakes that occurred within weeks of each other—the Haitian event and a devastating quake that struck the South American country of Chile on February 27, 2010. The Chilean earthquake measured 8.8, several hundred times more powerful than the tremor that struck Haiti. Chilean officials listed 486 deaths from the earthquake and accompanying tsunami. More than a half-million homes and thousands of businesses were destroyed. Damage, estimated at close to $30 billion, was more than double Haiti's financial losses.

Despite its severity, there was very little in the way of an international response to the Chilean tragedy. Chile did not ask for assistance. In the weeks following the quake, media coverage all but vanished. (In contrast, many months after the Haitian disaster, it remained a focus of frequent media attention.) Proud Chileans picked up the pieces of their shattered lives and went about the business of cleaning up, fixing up, and rebuilding.

How can the sharp differences in the way the two countries responded to their respective tragedies be explained? A stable and responsible government is essential if a country and its people are to prosper. During recent decades, Chile has had a stable democratic government. The newly elected president had been in office less than two weeks when the earthquake struck, yet the government was prepared to respond immediately and in a highly organized manner to the tragedy. The country's market economy has allowed many of its people to prosper. Chile has one of South America's largest (as a percent of the population) socioeconomic middle classes. Its people are well educated; the country has a sound education system and boasts a literacy rate of nearly 96 percent. When disaster strikes Chile, as it has on numerous occasions, the government and the country's citizens are prepared to respond in a prompt and resourceful manner.

Impoverished Haiti, on the other hand, is poorly prepared and inadequately equipped to cope with a disaster of any kind. The government's response to the tragedy was slow, disorganized, and largely ineffective. Disaster-relief plans were poor or lacking entirely. According to one international observer, "[T]he government in Port-au-Prince has lapsed into the classic pattern of corruption, inefficiency, and delay that holds the country hostage." The postquake Haitian response can best be described as marked by "chaos and corruption." Most leadership came from international agencies and various foreign groups. Unlike Chile and Chileans, Haiti and Haitians simply lack the ability to respond quickly and positively to a disaster.

CHAPTER

4

Historical Geography

Geographer Erhard Rostlund once wrote that "[t]he present is the fruit of the past and contains the seeds of the future." This wisdom is true for all nations, but it holds special meaning for Haiti. Few countries in the world have been more influenced by their past, or seen their future more clouded by historical conditions and events. In this chapter, you will learn why Rostlund's observation holds such important meaning for this poor and struggling Caribbean country.

Many people have questioned how two countries on one island—Haiti and the Dominican Republic—can be so different. Explaining such differences is the work of historical geography. For example, Haiti was colonized by France, whereas the Dominican Republic was a Spanish colony. Haiti's early population was composed mainly of slaves from Africa; the Dominican Republic had very few slaves. Two centuries ago, most Europeans were killed or left Haiti because of slave revolts; many Spaniards, however, remained in the Dominican Republic. There are many other differences between the two lands and peoples. (Present-day differences can be compared using the easily accessible data in the *CIA World Factbook.*)

PRE-COLUMBIAN HAITI

The earliest inhabitants of Hispaniola were Amerindians. They are believed to have moved into the Caribbean islands from tropical South America several thousand years ago. Known as Taino, the people spoke Arawak (a term also used to identify the Taino). The name by which most peoples identify themselves often reflects the group's highly positive self-image. The Taino were no exception. Their name means "noble" or "good." Taino peoples were found throughout much of the Caribbean. In addition to Hispaniola, they inhabited Cuba, Puerto Rico, Jamaica, and some of the smaller islands of the Lesser Antilles. The name *Haiti* comes from the Taino word *Ayiti*, meaning "land of high mountains."

The Taino were a gentle, peaceful village people who had a close-knit tribal society. There were five major Taino kingdoms on Hispaniola, and they lived in harmony with one another. Each was headed by a *cacique,* or chief. His position was inherited and his subjects paid him tribute (a form of tax). Polygamy was practiced, and many men had 2 or 3 wives. The cacique, however, often had as many as 30 wives. Both his wives and children were held in very high prestige in the patriarchal (male-dominated) Taino society.

All Taino lived in large houses called *bohíos*, although those of the caciques and commoners were quite different. Caciques' homes were rectangular in shape. They were large, built to accommodate the chief's huge family of up to 100 wives and children. Commoners also lived in large bohíos, but theirs were circular in shape. Each house held 10 to 15 families, with multiple wives and many children. Given the size of the families, these buildings might also easily accommodate 100 people. Houses were built of poles, straw, and palm fronds (leaves). Furnishings were sparse and generally limited to chairs and simple mats. People slept in hammocks, which were first made and used by Amerindians in Middle America (perhaps by the Mayans).

For food, the Taino farmed, fished, and hunted. Crops were raised on *conucos,* large man-made mounds that were covered with leaves to protect the soil from erosion. They grew a variety of crops. Cassava (manioc), a tuber, was their main food crop. Cassava is unique because it is poisonous unless processed. The tubers were processed into an oatmeal-like substance and soaked. The liquid, which included the poison, was then squeezed from the mixture. The remaining gruel was made into flour and baked as large flat-bread cakes. Other crops included maize (Indian corn), beans, squash, and peppers, all of which originated in Middle America. From South America came sweet potatoes, peanuts, and several types of fruit. Cotton and tobacco were also grown. There were few large wild animals on Hispaniola. Meat protein came from edible rodents, birds, turtles, snakes, worms, and most anything else that could be hunted or collected. Coastal Taino had large boats and were excellent fishermen. Sturdy nets were made from homegrown cotton.

The Taino on Hispaniola lived well, and their numbers grew to as many as 3 million according to some estimates. Most experts, however, place the figure much lower, perhaps 400,000 people. What is known is that the Amerindians were not immune to European diseases. Smallpox, malaria, and even many of our common childhood diseases took a dreadful toll on the native populations, as did being enslaved to work the mines and fields. Within a decade of the Spaniards' arrival, the population had plummeted to around 60,000. By 1531 the number had shrunk to about 600. It was not long thereafter that the last of the native population vanished from Hispaniola forever. Other than some archaeological remains, there is no trace of the Taino once having lived in Haiti. Strangely, today's Haitian culture is almost exclusively African and European. Few, if any, Taino cultural practices were passed down. Perhaps their major contribution lives on in the country's name, *Ayiti,* or Haiti.

COLUMBUS AND THE SPANISH ERA

Christopher Columbus landed on Hispaniola's north shore on December 5, 1492. It was his third landfall in the Americas. His first landing, on October 12, is believed to have been on San Salvador (also called Watling), a small island in the outer Bahamas. He also landed on Cuba's northeastern coast before reaching Hispaniola, where he built a small fort. Because the settlement was founded on December 24, he named it La Navidad (Christmas). The small settlement housed about 40 sailors from the *Santa Maria,* one of Columbus's vessels that sank in the Atlantic off Haiti's northern coast. Columbus named the island La Isla Española ("The Spanish Island"), later changed to Hispañola, or, in the English version, Hispaniola. He also claimed the island for the Spanish Crown.

Columbus returned to Spain and did not stay at La Navidad during the winter of 1492–1493. When he returned in 1493 with 17 ships and about 1,200 men, he found La Navidad in ruins with no sign of survivors. Although the Spaniards' disappearance remains a mystery, it is assumed that they were killed by Taino warriors. For this and other reasons, Columbus decided to move his settlement. He selected a location on the south side of the island, near the present-day site of Santo Domingo, capital of the Dominican Republic. Santo Domingo therefore became the first (and is now the oldest) continuously inhabited European city in the Americas.

The Spanish presence in present-day Haiti was short-lived. By the 1530s, rich deposits of gold and silver had been discovered in Middle and South America. Spain's attention immediately shifted to the mainland and its greater wealth. Haiti was all but abandoned. Most of the Spaniards remaining on Hispaniola were clustered in and around Santo Domingo. This historical reality resulted in a very sharp cultural division between today's Haiti and the Spanish-dominated Dominican Republic. One can only wonder what Haiti's past and present would be had the Spaniards at La Navidad not disappeared.

With Spain's success in finding wealth on the mainland, vessels carrying vast treasures of gold and silver began to sail through the Windward Passage, the narrow passageway between eastern Cuba and western Hispaniola. From most Spanish-settled Caribbean ports, it was the shortest route to Spain. Soon, French, Dutch, and British pirates established bases in present-day Haiti. They found the ships and their rich cargo of precious metal to be easy prey. The French, in particular, established a foothold in western Hispaniola and on several other islands. For nearly a century, much of western Hispaniola was little more than a wild no-man's land. Spain, having lost interest in the rugged western third of the island, turned the area over to France in 1697. Today, there is little trace of Spanish influence in Haiti. That which does exist is much more the result of influences spilling over from the Spanish-speaking Dominican Republic than from early Spanish settlement in the region.

THE FRENCH ERA

French pirates were based on the island of Tortuga, off the northwest tip of Haiti, by 1625. They pirated Spanish vessels and hunted wild cattle that originated with the sixteenth-century Spanish occupation of Hispaniola. (Nearly all the livestock in the Americas originated in Asia and was introduced into the New World by European settlers.) What they did with the cattle gave us a common word for pirates: *buccaneer*. To preserve the meat in the hot tropical environment, the French smoked it. The French word *boucanier* refers to "one who smokes meat."

In 1659 King Louis XIV commissioned the first official French settlement on Tortuga. Within two decades, the French, led by the French West India Company, gained unofficial control over the western third of Hispaniola. They named their new colony Saint Domingue. Today's Cap Haitien, the largest city on Haiti's north coast, was settled in 1670. Thus, it become the first French community on the mainland. When Spain officially ceded present-day Haiti to the French in 1697, yet another important step had been taken in molding Haiti's strong French cultural character.

PLANTATIONS AND SLAVERY

French planters were attracted to the new colony by the tropical climate and fertile soils of the coastal plain and river valleys. Initially, tropical plantation crops included cotton, cacao, tobacco, and indigo (a plant that yields blue dye). By the early 1700s, sugarcane and coffee were added to the list of plantation-grown crops.

As was true elsewhere in tropical environments, the Europeans had no taste for strenuous, back-breaking labor under the sweltering sun. Early attempts to enslave Amerindians were largely unsuccessful. European-introduced diseases took a horrible toll on native populations. Also, it was easy for the Taino slaves to escape and seek refuge in the rugged mountainous terrain, with which they were intimately familiar. Thus began the African slave trade, which certainly was one of the most inhumane chapters in the history of the Americas.

Figures on the African slave trade are extremely unreliable, with estimates ranging from around 6 million to more than 30 million. During the late 1700s, it is estimated that Saint Domingue had a slave population of nearly 800,000, or 25 slaves to each European (the white population at the time was about 32,000). This would have been roughly one-third of the entire Atlantic slave trade during the latter part of the eighteenth century. During the peak of the slave trade, as

Buccaneers fish for turtles in Haiti in 1571 in this historical illustration. The French pirates got their name from their practice of smoking meat to preserve it.

many as 40,000 Africans a year were brought to the colony. The slaves were not a homogeneous group. They came from many different West African locations and from hundreds of different tribes. They spoke many different languages, held many different beliefs (including Voodoo), and practiced many different customs.

So successful was the plantation economy of Saint Domingue that it earned the nickname "Pearl of the Antilles." Massive wealth was generated by the slave-based plantation economy. According to various sources, in the late 1760s the colony exported more than 120 million pounds (54.4 million kg) of raw and refined sugar to European markets. It also shipped 2 million pounds (907,184 kg) of cotton and 1 million pounds (453,592 kg) of indigo annually. By the late eighteenth century, Saint Domingue produced about 60 percent of all the coffee and 40 percent of all the sugar consumed throughout Europe.

All production, it must be remembered, was the result of slave labor, and for the slaves, conditions were horrendous (according to some scholars, they were the worst—by far—of any colony in the Americas). The following passage, written by a former slave, describes in gory detail the inhumane punishments experienced by some slaves:

> Have they not hung up men with heads downward, drowned them in sacks, crucified them on planks, buried them alive, crushed them in mortars? Have they not forced them to eat excretement [sic]? And, having flayed them with the lash, have they not cast them alive to be devoured by worms, or onto anthills, or lashed them to stakes in the swamp to be devoured by mosquitoes? Have they not thrown them into boiling cauldrons of cane syrup? Have they not put men and women inside barrels studded with spikes and rolled them down mountainsides into the abyss? Have they not consigned these miserable blacks to man-eating dogs until the latter, sated by human flesh, left the mangled victims to be finished off with bayonet . . . ?

Many slaves were able to flee the plantations, finding refuge in the rugged mountains. These escapees were called Maroons. Saint Domingue also had the largest and wealthiest free *gens de couleur* population ("people of color") in the Caribbean. (Today this term also applies to blacks, but at the time, it signified people of mixed racial background.) The people of color held middle-class status. Socially and economically they were sandwiched between French colonists and the African slaves. A number of them became quite successful economically. In fact, by 1789 they owned an estimated one-quarter of the slaves and about one-third of the land in Saint Domingue.

STEPS TOWARD INDEPENDENCE

Toward the end of the eighteenth century, conditions in Saint Domingue deteriorated rapidly. The French Revolution, which broke out in Europe in 1789, had a major impact on Saint Domingue. The French were too occupied with troubles at home to pay any attention to their distant colonies. Left alone, various factions in Saint Domingue quickly began to quibble among themselves. Tensions grew and by 1790, heated civil conflicts began to break out in the colony. One extremely hot issue was the claim by people of color that they were French citizens. This claim to full legal and political rights outraged the wealthy and powerful whites who held power in Saint Domingue. Slaves became increasingly frustrated and militant, and conditions continued to deteriorate. On August 22, 1791, slaves in the northern part of the colony revolted. The revolt, led by Toussaint Louverture, marked the beginning of the Haitian Revolution.

In 1792 France sent a representative to Saint Domingue in the hope of ending the conflict. He was there to stabilize the colony and ensure that France maintained control of its lucrative tropical possession. By then, the French National Convention had granted social equality to free people of color, and the representative was also to make sure that that these rights were recognized and respected by the whites. In February 1794 the French National Convention voted to free the slaves in all French colonies. (Slaves in the United States were not freed until 1865, 71 years following the emancipation in French-held lands.) This was a cruel blow to the plantation owners. In Saint Domingue, resistance to the French law grew. It involved white colonists, who were joined by some British, and—strangely, perhaps—free men of color who also opposed the abolition of slavery.

Toussaint Louverture (*above*), who played a leading role in the Haitian Revolution, is considered the father of Haiti.

By 1796 conditions had worsened. Former slaves were now armed, and British forces had stepped into the fray. It was here that Toussaint-Louverture (and others) and his battle-ready former slaves took command. Toussaint and his troops were successful in driving out the British in 1798. A year later he defeated the army representing the free people of color. By 1801, Toussaint had conquered Spanish Santo Domingo (today's Dominican Republic) and had freed that colony's slaves.

Following his victories, Toussaint made a bold decision that remains controversial and is still hotly debated by historians and others. He did not seek reprisal against the whites. According to writer C.L.R. James, Toussaint believed that "a population of slaves recently landed from Africa could not attain to civilization by 'going it alone.'" This is a very important point to remember in regard to Haiti's political and economic conditions. Toussaint, although black, realized that the soon-to-be independent country would have to depend upon the experience and expertise of Europeans if it were to be successful.

By 1802 France was once again able to turn attention to its colonial holdings. In the case of Saint Domingue, the response was to invade the colony with 40,000 troops. Toussaint was tricked into capture and deported to France, where he died. Here, however, nature, which is so often unkind to Haiti, played a very important role. With the onset of the rainy season, yellow fever and malaria began to ravage the French invaders. By the end of 1802, 80 percent of the French soldiers had died or were hospitalized.

In 1802 French leader Napoleon Bonaparte signed a law reestablishing slavery in some locations and stripping people of color of their recently gained rights. Although the slavery issue did not apply to Saint Domingue, many local leaders believed that it did. Fearing that slavery might be reinstated, the colony's black population fought back with even greater purpose and ferocity. Atrocities and deaths mounted. The retaliating French forces were unbelievably brutal. Captured blacks were hanged, drowned, burned alive, boiled, buried with insects, and subjected to countless other horrendous acts of torture. Blacks were equally brutal, torturing and killing captured whites and people of color. Ultimately, however, blacks and people of color joined forces against their common enemy, the ruthless French. In 1803 France and Britain once again were engaged in heated warfare against each other, which diverted France's attention from its Caribbean colonies. In November of that year, the French army in Saint Domingue was finally defeated once and for all.

Saint Domingue was now free to seek its own destiny, but historical events had imposed a number of seemingly insurmountable problems. Society, for example, was sharply divided. The vast majority of people were poverty-stricken, powerless former slaves. There were a small number of rich and powerful landowners. In between were a few people of color, who were viewed with suspicion and often contempt by both blacks and whites.

INDEPENDENT HAITI

On January 1, 1804, black freedom fighter Jean-Jacques Dessalines declared Haiti's independence from France and established himself as the new country's first emperor. (France did not formally recognize Haiti's independence until 1825, and it was not until 1862 that the United States formally recognized the country.) Haiti thus became the world's first black-governed republic. It is also the second-oldest independent state in the Americas. Only the United States, which gained independence from Great Britain in 1776, is older.

Many people suggest that today's less developed countries are poor because they once were colonies. Of course, this is not true. The United States, Canada, Australia, New Zealand, and all of Latin America were colonies at one time. A lack of political stability and economic development must be explained in some way other than former colonial status. The answer lies in cultural knowledge and experience, both of which develop slowly over decades, if not centuries. At the time of independence, and even today, Haitians had little experience in democratic self-governing. As a result, their economy remains stagnant.

TWO CENTURIES OF FRUSTRATION

By the time Haiti became independent in 1804, nearly all the foundation blocks upon which the country's future was built were in place.

Haiti has enjoyed brief periods of stability and prosperity, particularly during the latter part of the nineteenth century, but most of the country's history can best be described by the words *chaos*, *poverty*, and *corruption*. You will recall that Dessalines, Haiti's first leader, established himself as emperor, and in that role he held absolute power. Haitian politics has been marked by a long series of emperors, kings, presidents-for-life (a president-for-life has no term limit), and ruthless dictators. Even the democratically elected presidents of recent years have been dismal failures in the eyes of many Haitians (and others). Removal from office has been by force (coup d'état) far more often than by peaceful transition. The country's early prosperity is but a dim memory, as it has been for decades.

First, unlike Toussaint, Dessalines sought to rid Haiti of its remaining European population. Following the onset of black control, most of the French fled the country, going to Louisiana, Cuba, other French Caribbean possessions, or elsewhere. Dessalines captured and slaughtered 2,000 of those whites who remained. The decision to rid Haiti of its white population is cited by many as a primary cause for the country's present-day political and economic instability. It denied Haiti the knowledge and experience that had developed over centuries in Europe. The former slaves had no leadership experience in democratically governing themselves, and they had never been involved in the workings of a modern commerce-based economy. It is extremely important to recognize that this was a *cultural* problem, one of learning and experience, and one that persists unless people are taught otherwise. The differences are explained by the different cultural histories, respectively, of Western Europe and Africa. It has absolutely nothing to do with racial (biological) heritage.

Second, from the outset, Haiti has had a sharply divided society. There have always been a very small number of well-educated, rich, and powerful people. During the sixteenth century, they were primarily whites; during the seventeenth and eighteenth centuries, whites and people of color were the elite; since independence in 1804, blacks have held power. The vast majority of Haitians, however, have always been poor and powerless. This continues to be true today. Poverty, it can be said, breeds poverty. For Haiti, it is very difficult to build from a weak and crumbling foundation.

Third, education and experience are the keys to economic success and (at least to a degree) political stability. Even today, only about half of all Haitians are able to read and write, the lowest percentage in the Western Hemisphere. This is a legacy of the socially stratified (and still segregated) society in which the rich saw no need to educate the poor.

Fourth, in most countries, cities are the engines that power economic and other forms of development. From the earliest period of settlement, the majority of Haitians have been tied to the land. First they were slaves working the plantations. After their emancipation, they became rural peasants who tried to eke out a living from the land. Most Haitians, even today, are squatters who do not own the land on which they live.

CHAPTER

5

People and Culture

In 2006 Haiti took its first census in 24 years. It was only the fourth organized population count in the country's (then) 202-year history. The results were very disturbing. In nearly every negative category, Haiti ranked first (or last) among Western Hemisphere countries. A comprehensive census is any country's primary source of data. It provides a "snapshot" of the population in terms of its many characteristics. In this chapter, you will learn about Haiti's people. It begins with a look at the country's demographics (demography is the science that studies population statistics) and settlement (where people live). You also will learn about who the people are in terms of their racial ancestry and ethnicity. Finally, you will find out what the Haitians are like in terms of basic aspects of their culture (way of life).

POPULATION

There are two very important things to keep in mind as you read the sections of this chapter devoted to population and settlement. First, in a poor country such as Haiti, census data, at best, are little more than estimates. Figures vary widely and should be used only as a general guide to conditions. Second, most census data changed dramatically with the January 2010 earthquake. An estimated 2 to 3 percent of the country's people died in the quake or from injuries or disease in the months following. Others left Haiti as refugees from the disaster. Settlement, too, changed drastically as a result of the tragic event.

Most sources place Haiti's population at just over 9 million. According to the current *CIA World Factbook*, in mid-2010 Haiti's population was 9,035,536. Other estimates range from 8.9 to 9.7 million.

Population Change

Four factors determine whether a country's population grows, declines, or remains unchanged: births, deaths, in-migration, and out-migration. With as many as 300,000 deaths resulting directly or indirectly from the earthquake, certainly Haiti's population has declined. Additionally, an unknown number of Haitians emigrated (left the country) following the quake.

There are several ways to determine a country's changes in population. Perhaps the most common is the rate of natural (population) increase, or RNI. The RNI is determined by a country's birthrates and death rates. Haiti experienced 31 births and 10 deaths per 1,000 people during 2009. Both figures are the highest in the Americas. Estimates of the country's RNI varied between 1.84 and 2.1 percent per year in 2009. This figure is based upon *natural* conditions—births over deaths—and does not include migration. Although the earthquake will result in a drastic one-year drop in the RNI, the rate of gain has been fairly constant during recent years. It is nearly twice the world average increase of 1.15 percent.

Haitian immigrants wave U.S. flags after taking the oath of citizenship. Haiti is rapidly losing its population to other countries.

It is also one of the highest in the Americas and far ahead of the RNI for the United States (0.98 percent) and Canada (0.82 percent).

The total fertility rate (TFR) is another way to measure a country's population change. This figure is the average number of children to which a woman gives birth during her reproductive years. For Haiti, the TFR is 3.8, well above the world average of 2.5, and far greater than that of the United States (2.0) and Canada (1.6). The replacement level is 2.1 (the 0.1 is explained by the fact that some women will never give birth). Haitian women give birth to more children than those of almost any other country in the Americas.

Finally, migration can add to or reduce a country's population. Because of widespread poverty and, more recently, several major natural disasters, Haiti has a high rate of out-migration

(−2.07 per 1,000 people). This means that nearly 19,000 more people leave Haiti each year than migrate to the country. Following the catastrophic 2010 earthquake, the figure surely will increase drastically. In 2009, it was estimated that nearly 2 million Haitians lived outside their country. Greatest numbers were in the Dominican Republic (800,000), the United States (600,000), and Canada (100,000).

Only a few countries in the Americas are losing population to out-migration, yet experiencing a whopping RNI. In the case of Haiti, this is a reflection of the country's incredibly poor economy. As a general rule, widespread poverty and low levels of education go hand in hand with high fertility rates and rates of natural population increase. Haiti is no exception. When a country's population grows at a rate greater than its economy, the people become poorer. For a very long time, this situation has been a major problem for Haitians. Year after year, the country's population growth has simply outstripped its economic gains.

Demographics of Well-being

A number of demographic figures can provide clues to the well-being experienced by a country's population. Perhaps the most reliable is life expectancy, the average number of years a person is expected to live. The average life span is a good indicator of many other conditions. For example, it reflects health, income, education, safety, environmental quality, and much more. As is true of most Haitian demographic data, the picture is bleak. Haitians, on average, live about 61 years (males 59 years and females 63 years). This is the shortest life span in the Americas, and by an alarming margin of 5 years. The world average is about 66 years; in the United States and Canada, the life expectancy is 78 and 81 years, respectively.

Another important clue to human well-being is a country's age structure. Population pyramids (see Figure 2) offer a visual image of age and sex divisions of a country's population. As is

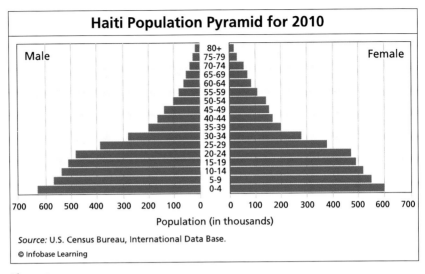

Haiti Population Pyramid for 2010

Male / Female

Age groups: 80+, 75-79, 70-74, 65-69, 60-64, 55-59, 50-54, 45-49, 40-44, 35-39, 30-34, 25-29, 20-24, 15-19, 10-14, 5-9, 0-4

700 600 500 400 300 200 100 0   0 100 200 300 400 500 600 700

Population (in thousands)

Source: U.S. Census Bureau, International Data Base.

© Infobase Learning

Figure 2

the case in nearly all less-developed lands, Haiti's population is young. The median age is 21.1 (versus 37 for the United States and 40 for Canada), and 38 percent of the population is under 15 years of age. In the Americas, only impoverished Guatemala has a younger population. On the other hand, only 3.4 percent of Haitians are 65 or older. Again, this figure is much lower than that of nearly any other Western Hemisphere country.

Infant mortality rate is still another valid indicator of a country's standard of living. It is the annual number of deaths among children from birth to one year of age. For Haiti, the figure is particularly shocking. Of 1,000 live births, 60 infants will die during their first year (compared to the world average of 46). No other country in the Americas can match this horrendous figure. Several factors contribute to the high infant mortality rate. They include inadequate medical facilities and personnel; midwives, rather than trained physicians, attend most births. Sanitation facilities are poor, with most Haitians lacking access to clean water and adequate sewage disposal. Many youngsters suffer from inadequate diets. Each of these conditions worsens in the rural environment where half of all Haitians live.

Demographic data, as you have seen, can tell us much more than just numbers. They give a revealing glimpse of the well-being of a country's population. This in turn tells us a great deal about a country's human development. The UN has created the Human Development Index (HDI), a measure of human well-being. The HDI compares education, literacy, life expectancy, living standards, and other conditions among countries. Using this measure, Haiti's position is a dismal 145 among the world's 169 countries ranked in 2010. This ranking, too, is the lowest in the Americas (the next lowest is Guatemala, ranked 116).

Haiti clearly has a long way to go before its population can enjoy a scale of living comparable to that of other Western Hemisphere countries. (Scale of living is what people actually have; standard of living refers to their goals, or what they would like to have.) If the country is to achieve this goal, the government faces two huge challenges. First, health care and sanitation must be vastly improved. Second, the population must be better educated. Just over half of all Haitians over the age of 15 are able to read and write. Both improvements will be very costly. Obviously, with an inept government, massive corruption, and the hemisphere's poorest economy, Haiti faces a long uphill struggle to improve the living conditions of its people.

SETTLEMENT

There are about 9 million Haitians. That is the country's population. The term *settlement* refers to the way in which people are distributed across the land they occupy. Using the "official" figure, Haiti's population density is about 840 people per square mile (323 per square kilometer). Such figures, however, are all but meaningless. In the area affected by the earthquake, including Port-au-Prince, conditions are extremely crowded, with densities measured in the thousands per square mile. Before the earthquake, nearly one-third of all Haitians—about

3.5 million of them (38 percent of the country's population)—lived in the metropolitan area of the capital. In some of the more remote mountainous areas, the population density is very low. Most of the population is sandwiched into urban centers and areas with fertile soils, such as valleys and coastal plains. Mountainous areas tend to support low populations.

Looking at settlement another way, about half the population lives in cities (47 percent) and about half is rural (53 percent), living scattered about the countryside. Interestingly, these figures are very close to those for literacy, also about 50 percent. Most city people have at least some education. On the other hand, schools are few and far between in the country's rural areas. Many youngsters living in the countryside simply do not have schools to attend.

During recent years, the pace of rural-to-urban migration has increased rapidly. Between 2005 and 2010, the country's urban population grew at an annual rate of about 4.5 percent. This trend is widespread throughout the less-developed world. People are drawn to cities where they have much better access to wage-paying jobs, basic services, and other amenities and opportunities. It is difficult to determine, however, what effect the earthquake had on urban versus rural settlement.

RACIAL ANCESTRY AND ETHNICITY

Dividing people into different categories based upon biological and cultural characteristics is becoming more and more difficult. Today, the world's population is becoming increasingly mixed in terms of race and ethnicity, making such divisions rather meaningless. Nevertheless, three distinctions have been commonly used to divide people into categories: race, culture (ethnicity), and nationality.

Race refers to one's biological makeup. It is a vague and meaningless concept that most social scientists (and others) long ago discarded. Culture is learned human behavior and defines a people's way of life. (The term *ethnicity* is often used in the place of culture.) Nationality is a rather complex and often misused concept and term. If you were in a foreign country and someone asked what you are, how would you answer? Most people would identify their country of residence, but not all. Some Canadians, for example, might answer in a way that would reflect their French heritage or their residence in French Quebec. It is important to remember that one race of people can represent many cultures and nationalities; a single culture can include people of many races and nationalities; and a single nationality, such as American or Canadian, often includes people of many different races and cultures (ethnicities).

When Europeans first arrived on Hispaniola, the island was home to a rather large Amerindian population. Most of the native peoples died within decades, many from European-introduced diseases against which they had no natural immunity. Others were killed in skirmishes with the European intruders. Today, Haiti has a rather homogeneous population. About 95 percent of the people are blacks who trace their distant ancestry to Africa. Another 4 percent of Haitians are of mixed black and white ancestry, the people of color. Whites are a very small minority, numbering less than 1 percent of the population. Most of the white population is Arab or West European in origin. There also are a small number of East Indians and Chinese.

CULTURE

Haitian culture (way of life) offers a rich mix of traits contributed through time mainly by Amerindians, Africans (from various tribes), the Spanish, and the French. Combined, they have created Haiti's distinctive religion, language, social interactions, foodways, customs, and other practices. In terms of major institutions and practices, the French (colonial) imprint is evident in the country's language and religion. In many other cultural aspects, African traits dominate. In this section, attention is focused upon language and religion.

Language

French is one of Haiti's two official languages. It is the language spoken and written by nearly all well-educated people, and it is used in government, education, and most formal business activities. But even if you speak fluent French, don't expect to understand the Haitian version of the language. Languages change when their speakers are separated for long periods of time (in this case, several centuries) from the main body of speakers. The French spoken in Louisiana or Quebec, for example, is quite different from what one would hear in Paris. So it is in Haiti.

The second language is Haitian Creole, which is spoken by almost everyone. Creole evolved out of necessity during the seventeenth century. People speaking many different languages had to develop a tongue that they could use in common. The situation is not unique. Hundreds of different Creole languages are spoken in various countries throughout much of the world. On Hispaniola, there were Spanish and French speakers, along with the native Taino. The Africans brought to the island as slaves spoke dozens of different West African languages. On several of the offshore islands, there were English- and Dutch-speaking pirates and buccaneers. Haitian Creole is a language that grew as a mix of words, grammar, and syntax (the way words are used in a sentence) borrowed from many tongues.

Because neighboring Dominican Republic is Spanish-speaking, some Haitians also speak Spanish. A substantial number of educated people also speak English. This is particularly true of those involved in international economic activities, including tourism.

Religion

Because of its early French cultural influence, Haiti is dominantly Roman Catholic. Catholicism is the official state religion, as established by the country's constitution. About 80 percent of the population professes to be Catholic, although

Haitian Roman Catholics take part in the annual pilgrimage at Morne Calvaire on Good Friday. Catholicism is the official religion, although some citizens practice other religions.

the number of active churchgoers is much lower. Sixteen percent of Haitians are Protestant, most of whom belong to various evangelical denominations. There are also a number of Latter Day Saints (Mormons). Only 1 percent of all Haitians claim no religious affiliation whatsoever.

About half of Haiti's population practices Voodoo, which has been elevated to the status of an official religion in the country. Despite its being recognized as a religion, many Haitians hold two faiths, both Christian and Voodoo.

Voodoo was created in Haiti by African slaves in the 1500s. The Africans arrived in Haiti with their own traditional religious beliefs, but the French slave owners forced them to convert to Roman Catholicism. As such, Voodoo is a syncretic faith (a faith that incorporates features of several religions); it is a mixture of many beliefs, including Roman Catholic, West African, and even some Amerindian influences. Similar religions include New Orleans (Louisiana) Voodoo, Candomblé and Umbanda in Brazil, and Arará and Santería in Cuba.

Characteristics of the faith are far too numerous and complex to describe in a short space. In brief, *vodouisants* (those who believe in Voodoo) worship deities called *Lwa*. They venerate (worship) the dead and have means by which they attempt to protect against evil. As is true of many "different" religious or other practices, Voodoo is surrounded by myths and misconceptions. For example, at least in the Haitian version, very little witchcraft is practiced. Haitians do not stick pins in dolls or photographs to avenge perceived misdeeds against them!

The foregoing passages merely touch upon some of the most basic elements of Haitian culture. In this chapter, you have learned that a close relationship exists between population and human well-being. The latter, in turn, is strongly influenced by a country's government and economy, the topics discussed in the following chapter.

6

Politics and Economy

Haiti has been plagued by political violence and instability throughout most of its history. When one looks about the world in an attempt to explain poverty, three factors stand out. The first is political instability. If a country is poorly governed, its economy almost certainly will also be poorly developed. Second in importance is the economic system. If people are not free to pursue their economic goals in a free and open market, their country and its people will almost always be impoverished. Finally, there can be little economic progress when corruption is rampant within a country. In each arena, Haitians have long suffered under conditions that have contributed to the country's incredible poverty. By almost any measure, it is the politically least stable, economically least developed, and most corrupt country in the Western Hemisphere.

Imagine that you have a billion dollars to invest. You plan to build a huge factory in some foreign country. As a humanitarian, you have decided to invest your capital in a less-developed country (LDC). You want to help people by creating thousands of jobs with fair wages. Certainly this will boost the country's struggling economy. But there are many LDCs. Where should you build? As you begin to check out possible sites, you immediately become aware of Haiti's desperate poverty—it is the poorest country in the Western Hemisphere. The country is attractive to you for several reasons. It has a large unemployed potential workforce. Also, it is close to the United States, a factor that would reduce shipping costs. But you soon learn that there are some major problems.

Because the country is impoverished, the infrastructure you need for your plant is poor to nonexistent. It would cost you millions of dollars to build the required facilities for transportation, water purification, and sewage disposal, among other needs, and you certainly would not want to depend upon Haiti's infamously unreliable electrical supply; you would have to build your own power installation. The government is unstable and corrupt beyond imagination. Leaders come and go, often by coup d'état, and you can't be sure who would be in power. In a bungling bureaucracy, clearing the way for your development would be painstakingly slow, perhaps taking years, and you have heard that absolutely nothing gets done without paying hefty bribes to officials.

The labor force is largely untrained and poorly educated. Nearly half the population, you learn, is unable to read or write. Working toward some long-term goal (like saving for a "rainy day" or retirement) has never dawned on most Haitians. And working an eight-hour day, five or six days a week, is a totally alien idea to many people living within the largely traditional folk economy. Oh, yes, and the country is frequently ravaged by destructive hurricanes and earthquakes.

Would you decide to invest your billion dollars in a country like that? If your answer is "No way!" you are well on your way to understanding at least some of the problems Haiti faces in developing its economy.

A HISTORY OF POLITICAL INSTABILITY

Since gaining independence in 1804, the country has enjoyed very few periods of political stability and economic prosperity. As historical events have shown time and time again, good (effective) government leads to a solid economy. On the other hand, bad government results in a poor economy. These realities are true almost without exception.

For a brief period during the latter part of the nineteenth century, there was a glimmer of hope for Haiti. Following the adoption of a new constitution in 1867, several peaceful transitions of government took place. The economy improved greatly, as did the condition of the Haitian people. The faith of the Haitian people in their government was restored. Outsiders, too, gained confidence in the country and began to invest in its economy. Primary industries such as sugar and rum prospered. For a period of time, Haiti actually became a model for economic growth in Latin America.

A half century of political stability and economic prosperity ended abruptly in 1911. Between 1911 and 1915 the country had six different presidents, all of whom either were killed while in office or fled the country. Nearly the entire twentieth century and the first decade of the twenty-first has been a political and economic nightmare for Haiti and its citizens. On several occasions, U.S. military forces have occupied the country in an attempt to stabilize conditions. Since 2004, a UN peacekeeping force, which includes U.S. and Canadian troops, has been in place to foster stability in the country.

The Period of U.S. Intervention (1911–1934)

Events of the past century can be roughly divided into three major periods, separated by short gaps of time. First was a period of foreign intervention that lasted from 1911 until 1934. By 1911 conditions in Haiti had deteriorated into near-total chaos. United States occupation forces (Marines) entered the country and basically gained control of Haiti's political, economic, and foreign affairs. Although the U.S. involvement was criticized by many, there were some positive contributions. For example, during the more than three decades of occupation, health, education, agriculture, and infrastructure (roads, electrical power, water delivery, and other necessities) were greatly improved, and there were several consecutive democratic elections. Following the withdrawal of U.S. forces in 1934, conditions began to deteriorate. Several presidents were unable to stabilize the country and were forced to leave office, and the economy began to falter.

The Duvalier Era (1957–1986)

The second era began in September 1957, when Dr. François "Papa Doc" Duvalier was elected president. Although democratically elected to office, Papa Doc very quickly established himself as still another Haitian dictator. By 1964, in fact, he had established himself as president-for-life. During his 14 years in office, he earned a reputation as being one of the most brutal and corrupt leaders in recent history. Political intimidation, including an estimated 30,000 murders of those who opposed his rule, marked Papa Doc's time in office. Officially, his paramilitary police—the dreaded Tonton Macoutes (named for a Voodoo monster)—carried out his brutal orders. Duvalier was quite popular among the country's black lower socioeconomic class. It was the mulatto elite he sought to destroy. As a result, many of Haiti's educated and economically successful people were either murdered or left the country.

François Duvalier died in 1971 and was followed in office by his totally inexperienced 19-year-old son, Jean-Claude "Baby Doc" Duvalier. Under Baby Doc's administration, the country's economic and political conditions continued to decline. He had little taste for the day-to-day matters of governing, most of which he turned over to his mother. Rather, Baby Doc was hard at work becoming an internationally recognized playboy and a master of corruption. Through various fraudulent schemes and by pillaging his country's meager coffers, he was able to amass a fortune estimated at close to a half-billion dollars.

By 1980 a number of circumstances came together to strengthen an increasingly vocal opposition to Duvalier and his regime. That year he married a mulatto divorcée in a $3 million ceremony. This upset many Haitians, who remembered his father's ruthless campaign against the mulatto elite. Because of Duvalier's pilfering of public funds, the government had but limited financial resources. There was little money left to build the economy or combat the various crises that were about to befall the country.

In the early 1980s Haiti was hit by an epidemic of African swine fever virus. Most rural peasants raised Creole pigs. They were the primary source of meat protein for rural people, and they could also be sold for cash that could be used to purchase necessities. To stop the spread of the disease, however, it was ordered that the pigs be slaughtered, which deprived rural people of their primary source of meat and income. At about the same time, Haiti was devastated by a widespread outbreak of HIV/AIDS, a disease from which an alarming number of Haitians still suffer. A final blow happened in 1983 when Pope John Paul II visited devoutly Roman Catholic Haiti. The pope strongly condemned Jean-Claude Duvalier and his regime, beginning a rebellion that finally forced Duvalier to resign in 1986. With an estimated half-billion pilfered dollars, he went into luxurious exile in France.

There is an almost unbelievable postscript to the Baby Doc Duvalier story. Following the 2010 earthquake, many if not most Haitians were very critical of the slow and inadequate response by the government, which was headed by René Préval. Many called for Duvalier to return and participate in the upcoming presidential election. According to the Haitian

Francois "Papa Doc" Duvalier is inaugurated in the National Palace in 1957. The brutal dictator's rule resulted in Haiti's brain drain—or the depletion of an educated, skilled upper class—which cost the nation considerably.

constitution, a presidential candidate must have resided in the country for the five years immediately preceding an election. In January 2011, Duvalier returned to Haiti to, in his words, "help my country." Two days after his arrival, he was formally charged with corruption, theft, and misappropriation of funds. Fortunately for Haitians, Baby Doc was deterred by the rule of law.

The Post-Duvalier Era (1986–present)

In 1987, a new Haitian constitution was ratified. It called for an elected president and bicameral (two-chambered) parliament. It also provided for a prime minister, cabinet, various ministers, and a supreme court, all appointed by the president with the consent of Parliament. As history has shown time and time again, a huge gap often exists between a country's constitution and the reality of its government. On Election Day in November 1987, for example, government troops killed as many as 300 voters. The political leaders had orchestrated the murders so they could cancel the election and stay in control. It worked. Another election was held in 1988, but it was boycotted by nearly all candidates, and because of voter intimidation only 4 percent of possible voters turned out. The person who won the election was ousted by the military after having served only several months in office.

For the most part, events of the past two decades have been more of the same. The United States has intervened on occasion in an attempt to ensure constitutional rule. On several occasions, former president Jimmy Carter has represented the U.S. government in Haiti (and elsewhere). These and other initiatives resulted in what, for Haiti, was a miracle. In February 1996 René Préval replaced Jean-Bertrand Aristide as president. Both had been elected in what was described by American and other outside observers as fair elections. This was the first time in history that Haiti had a successful transition between two democratically elected presidents. But in this case, the hope for peace and stability was a cruel mirage. By 2000 political chaos had returned, and it persisted throughout the first decade of the twenty-first century. Conditions deteriorated to the point that in 2004 the UN sent a peacekeeping force that included U.S. and Canadian troops into the country. They remain there today.

In 2006 former president René Préval was reelected to office, a position he continued to hold until he was replaced following an election held in early 2011. During much of his time in office, protests and demonstrations continued. Following the January 2010 earthquake, the government response was extremely weak and disorganized. Tensions once again began to grow to what may be a breaking point.

During its two centuries of independence, Haiti has rarely enjoyed political peace and stability. Governments have come and gone, more often by force than by ballot. Politically, Haiti faces many challenges, the greatest of which is to stick to its constitution. It also must overcome the tradition of leaders who grasp power far beyond that granted by the constitution. Corruption must be stopped. Far too often, leaders use their office to line their pockets from public funds. Haitians long for political stability that will encourage economic growth and prosperity for their country.

HAITI'S ECONOMY

Haiti's economy has been in shambles throughout most of the country's history. It is the weakest in the Western Hemisphere, and by a wide margin. There are many ways to measure economic development. In the Americas, Haiti ranks at the bottom in nearly all of them. Its people are extremely poor, and they grow increasingly frustrated with those conditions that hinder economic development. In many economic categories, conditions are getting worse, not better. The 2010 earthquake struck a crippling blow to the country's economy. Businesses, buildings, transportation routes, and people's dreams all collapsed with the tremor. It will take years for the country to return to even its dismal prequake economic level.

Regardless of the method used to measure its economy, Haiti ranks among the world's poorest and least developed nations. Economic data can and often do change quite rapidly. During recent years, for example, the world has experienced an economic downturn. Surprisingly, while this was occurring, Haiti's economy actually grew by a percent or so each year. Following the earthquake disaster, however, the country's economy surely will plunge. Much of the country's official records were destroyed by the earthquake, so most economic data will be little more than educated guesses for at least several years.

What is known is that the earthquake destroyed much of Haiti's economic infrastructure—the means of production, sales, and distribution. It will take years for the country to return to its predisaster level. Least hurt was agriculture; the earthquake struck Port-au-Prince and the immediate surrounding area, but left much of the country's farming area untouched. On a positive note, nearly $10 billion in aid has been pledged by various countries and agencies. Unfortunately, by some estimates only about 15 to 20 percent of the pledged money will actually be received. Any aid received will help the country rebuild, and rebuilding will create jobs. This is essential in a country where the preearthquake unemployment or underemployment rate was estimated to be two-thirds of the population. Fully 80 percent of the population lives below the poverty line. To make matters worse, an estimated 20 percent of those Haitians who were employed lost their jobs as a result of the earthquake.

The Grim Statistics

Economic statistics for Haiti vary greatly from source to source. Most data are extremely unreliable. Much of the following economic information is taken from the *CIA World Factbook* (2010) and reflects 2009 (preearthquake) statistics. The following figures, then, are presented simply to give you a general impression of just how desperate economic conditions are in Haiti.

One of the most widely used measures of a country's economy is its GDP, the annual value of all goods and services it produces during a one-year period. Estimates of Haiti's 2009 GDP range vary greatly from about $7 billion to nearly $12 billion. To give you some idea of comparison, Vermont ranks

Demonstrators shout "Down with Préval" to protest the Haitian president following the 2010 earthquake.

fiftieth among U.S. states in gross state product, yet Haiti's GDP is only about one-third to one-half that of Vermont's. This imbalance becomes even more obvious when one realizes that Vermont's population is about 620,000 and Haiti's is around 9 million. Haiti's GDP ranks 144 among the world's countries, but this figure is misleading. Many countries are much smaller in both size and population, and hence have smaller economies.

It is much more revealing to see how the GDP works out per individual. Looked at this way, Haiti's per capita GDP is far and away the lowest in the Americas; according to different sources, it ranges from $790 to $1,200 (2009). Using the higher figure, Haiti ranks 206 among the 229 countries listed. In the Western Hemisphere, Nicaragua is the second-poorest nation; yet it ranks 169 among the world's nations and has a per capita GDP of $2,800, more than twice that of Haiti.

There is a difference between a country's economic production and individual income. When the latter is considered, the figure for Haiti is even more depressing. The average per capita income is estimated to be just under $500. This means that the average Haitian has an income of about $1.40 per day! This figure is comparable to those in many of the poorer countries in Africa or Asia.

Haiti's distribution of wealth is a major source of social unrest and conflict. So far we have focused on Haiti's grinding poverty, but the country also has a very wealthy class of elites. Again, figures vary greatly from source to source, but it is clear that between 1 and 10 percent of the population hold about half the country's wealth. The poorest of the poor, the lowest 10 percent of the population, hold less than 1 percent of the wealth. This situation calls for an explanation. About half of all Haitians, it must be remembered, are rural farmers and unable to read and write. They are largely self-sufficient and may barter (trade) some form of labor for items they are unable to provide for themselves, much the way many Americans and Canadians lived a century or more ago. Today, the Haitians are poor by our standards, but many live quite comfortably based upon their expectations and needs and their ability to provide for themselves in a traditional folk economy.

Sources of Income

Haiti's economy is unique in still another way. Foreign aid makes up an estimated 30 to 40 percent of the government's budget. Most of the money comes from the United States, Canada, and the European Union. Promises of foreign aid increased greatly, to nearly $10 billion, following the earthquake. Another estimated 25 percent of the GDP comes from remittances, which is money sent home by the 2 million or so Haitians living abroad. Amazingly, remittances are the country's primary source of foreign exchange. Looked at another way, money sent by Haitians living abroad to relatives in Haiti amounts to nearly six times the country's annual export earnings!

For most countries, reliable data are available for contributions to the national economy by sector. This is not the case for Haiti. The most current (CIA) data are for 2004 and provide us with only a very general idea of productivity. At that time, services provided just over half of the GDP, or 52 percent. Agriculture followed with 28 percent, and industry contributed 20 percent. It is doubtful whether these figures have changed much. Following the earthquake, a drop certainly will occur in the contributions of both industry and services to the economy.

Much Haitian agriculture is subsistence; that is, people growing crops and raising animals for their own consumption. Commercially, coffee, sugar, rum, cacao, and mangoes are major agricultural exports. For reasons expressed earlier in the chapter, the industrial sector has never really developed, although the country has a rapidly expanding clothing industry, and garments account for two-thirds of all Haitian exports.

International Economic Ties

Among the world's countries, Haiti ranks very near the top in terms of dependence upon foreign assistance of various kinds. An estimated two-thirds of its "income" comes from aid and remittances. Exports account for between $500 and $600 million annually. This figure, however, pales in comparison to the just over $2 billion spent on imports. The country imports various manufactured goods, including machinery and transportation equipment. It also must import nearly all its fuel and other raw materials. This imbalance between imports and exports gives the country a whopping trade deficit, one of the world's highest.

The only way Haiti has been able to keep from going totally bankrupt is that the World Bank and other agencies have written off huge debts. In 2009, for example, $525 million of debt was forgiven. Clearly, the country is dependent upon foreign aid and its debts being written off. Yet because Haiti remains one of the world's most corrupt countries, many potential donors are increasingly hesitant to invest in the country. Political instability, a lack of security, and a very poor infrastructure also contribute to Haiti's dismal economic situation. Sadly, an improvement in the country's situation is not in sight. Both politically and economically, Haitians still are confronted by many very high mountains beyond mountains.

7

Living in
Haiti Today

L ife in Haiti has never been easy. Nature's wrath, poor political
    leadership, and abject poverty have been a part of life through-
    out much of the country's history. Poor and inadequate health
services, widespread illiteracy, and a lack of adequate infrastructure
also are a part of today's living for most Haitians. You have seen that
in the HDI Haiti ranks a dismal 145 among the world's 169 ranked
countries. The index uses a number of life-quality conditions to
determine a country's position. By a wide margin, Haiti holds the
lowest ranking of any country in the Americas. You have read many
statistics and descriptions of the bleak conditions in the country.
As you can imagine, life in Haiti today is extremely harsh for most
residents. They face a seemingly endless series of mountains beyond
mountains to climb in their struggle to live normal, peaceful, prosperous lives.

Any discussion of life in Haiti today, of course, must take into consideration the huge changes brought about by the January 2010 earthquake. In the affected area, the lives of nearly everyone changed dramatically. Of those residents who survived, most lost one or more relatives, friends, or neighbors, and most homes were destroyed or severely damaged. But away from the zone of destruction, life continues as it has for decades.

LIFE IN THE COUNTRYSIDE

About half of all Haitians live in the countryside. These are the people who, by and large, are living in a traditional folk culture and barter economy. When you read that approximately half of all Haitians live on about $1.00 a day, many if not most of them are these rural folk. Many of the rural people are illiterate. In the countryside, they never had an opportunity to attend school. There simply were no schools to attend, and even today there still are none in many places.

Facilities taken for granted in developed countries are often lacking in Haiti. Most rural homes, for example, have no electricity or access to a clean and reliable water supply. Sanitation facilities, such as adequate toilets and garbage disposal, are lacking. There are few communication facilities to link people with the outside world. The nearest health-care workers and facilities may be many miles away in the nearest city. Access to these and other urban amenities is difficult in a country where transportation linkages are primitive and, in many locations, nonexistent.

Charcoal is the primary fuel for cooking and heating. Because it is made from wood, Haiti is largely deforested and erosion is widespread. Because of the widespread deforestation, Haiti has one of the world's most devastated rural landscapes. A number of international and other agencies are attempting to introduce solar ovens as an alternative to charcoal use. These sun-powered cooking devices are inexpensive and quite effective.

As Haiti's rural population grows, so do the country's environmental problems. Most rural people depend upon subsistence farming. They grow crops and raise a few chickens, pigs, or other animals to feed their families. Most of the country's fertile soil, found in river valleys or on coastal plains, is used for commercial agriculture. Noncommercial subsistence agriculture, on the other hand, is found in the rugged terrain where most of Haiti's peasants live. About two-thirds of all Haitians are engaged in agriculture, yet farming contributes only about 28 percent of the country's GDP. This is because most agriculture is noncommercial. Farming on steep terrain and widespread deforestation in a rainy land are ingredients for disaster. Each year, Haiti loses more and more of its precious soil to erosion. As a result, it becomes increasingly difficult for rural people to eke out even a meager living.

URBAN LIVING

Throughout most of the world, cities offer greater opportunities, more amenities, and easier living than do rural places. This reality helps to explain the rural-to-urban migration pattern that has existed throughout much of the world during recent centuries. Simply stated, people are attracted to cities and what they offer. Sadly, the reality is that life in a city is not always better.

Slums surround nearly every large city in Latin America, including those in Haiti. Cité Soleil, for example, is a slum of nearly a half-million people in the Port-au-Prince metropolitan area. It is one of the largest and most crowded slums found anywhere in the Americas. Most of its people are dirt-poor and illiterate. According to a source cited by the International Red Cross, Cité Soleil is "a microcosm of all the ills in Haitian society: … [chronic] unemployment, illiteracy, non-existent public services, [u]nsanitary conditions, rampant crime, and armed violence." Following the earthquake, it took nearly two weeks for the first aid to arrive in the heavily damaged slum.

Because Haiti is depleting its natural resources, various agencies are working to help the country develop alternate energy sources. Above, a woman uses a solar oven instead of one fueled by charcoal.

Was this sad situation the result of a physical inability to reach the community, or was it something much deeper—a reflection of a lack of care for the country's poor and neglected people? Regardless of which is true, this kind of life and environment awaits many first-generation migrants to a city.

Roughly one-third of all Haitians lived in or near Port-au-Prince before the earthquake. The city was the country's heart and soul. Geographers refer to such a metropolis as a "primate city." It is an urban center that has the greatest population, and also is the country's political, economic, and cultural leader. Nearly all of Port-au-Prince was destroyed in the earthquake. Where, when, and even whether it will be rebuilt is anyone's guess. Certainly what rises in its place will be much different from the sprawling city before the disaster.

Including Port-au-Prince (current population unknown), Haiti has only five communities with populations over 100,000. Three of these cities—Carrefour, Delmas, and Pétionville—are located within the Port-au-Prince metropolitan area. Carrefour (about 440,000 people) is a sprawling slum, as well as a "bedroom community" from which many residents commute(d) to the capital for work. Much of the city was destroyed by the earthquake. Delmas (380,000 people) is a thriving industrial and commercial center, and Pétionville (110,000 people) is an eastern suburb and one of the richest areas in the entire country. Home to many businesspeople, diplomats, and wealthy citizens, Pétionville is one of Haiti's two major tourist destinations. The attractive town is perched on a hillside. Hotels, upscale restaurants and nightclubs, and many businesses that cater to the wealthy residents and international tourists line its streets.

The final winning question of the 2010 National Geographic Bee was "What is the largest city in northern Haiti?" The answer is Cap Haitien. The city of about 190,000 is located on the northern coast. In addition to its attractive Caribbean beaches, Cap Haitien offers many historic monuments, including the famous nearby Citadelle Laferrière. It is also recognized for its well-preserved French colonial architecture and quaint streets. Because of its various attractions and relative safety, the city shares with Pétionville the distinction of being one of the country's two tourist centers. It particularly attracts upper-class Haitian vacationers.

INFRASTRUCTURE

It may seem strange to have a section on infrastructure— roads, electricity, running water, sanitation systems, and so forth—in this chapter. To better understand and appreciate why it is included, consider the following: Imagine living with no roads, or only a primitive winding dirt trail. You have no electricity or running water, no sanitary sewage or garbage disposal. Well, this is what life in Haiti is like for a significant number of its rural and even many urban citizens who dwell in slums.

Haiti has a total of only 2,585 miles (4,160 kilometers) of roads, of which 628 miles (1,011 km) are paved. Large areas of the country are for all practical purposes inaccessible by road. There are only two major paved highways. One runs from Port-au-Prince northward, through Montrouis and Gonaïves, to Cap Haitien. The second extends westward from Port-au-Prince along the Southern Peninsula, passing through Léogâne and Petit Goâve, and ending at Les Cayes. The country has no railroads. There are about a dozen seaports, but only the Port International de Port-au-Prince and Port de Saint-Marc are able to accommodate large vessels and cargoes. Elsewhere, port facilities are in poor shape and of limited use. There are 14 airports, but only 4 have paved runways. Toussaint Louverture International Airport, located near Port-au-Prince, is the country's major air hub and jetport. Northern American airlines that serve Haiti are American, Delta, and Air Canada.

According to the Inter-American Development Bank, the largely government-owned electricity infrastructure in Haiti is in shambles. It faces a permanent crisis of major shortages and offers the poorest coverage of electrical service in the entire Western Hemisphere. Only about 12.5 percent of Haiti's population has regular access to electricity, a figure that rises to about 25 percent if illegal connections are included. A comparable percentage has access to a reliable water supply and adequate sanitation facilities.

EDUCATION

For any country to prosper, its people must be educated. Sadly, in terms of education Haiti also lags far behind all other countries in the Western Hemisphere. According to government figures, only about half of all Haitians (52.9 percent) can read and write. There are about 15,200 primary schools, about 90 percent of which are private. Most are owned and managed by religious groups, communities, or various other nongovernmental organizations.

An estimated 67 percent of Haitian youngsters are enrolled in primary schools, but less than 30 percent of the students who begin their schooling ever reach the sixth grade. The figure is even worse for secondary education, with only about 20 percent of eligible-age children enrolled. About 90 percent of students at all levels attend church-run schools. The percentage of youngsters attending school drops sharply in the countryside. Education is further hindered by a chronic shortage of qualified teachers and a lack of adequate educational facilities and supplies.

Haiti has several colleges and universities, but few Haitians can afford to attend them. Of those who do earn college degrees (whether in Haiti or abroad), an estimated 80 percent leave the country. This results in a very costly drain of talent. Haiti desperately needs well-educated people to help in development. Humans, after all, can and should be any country's most important resource.

HEALTH CARE

Only some 40 percent of Haitians have access to basic health care, a condition that has become even more desperate following the earthquake. The tremor destroyed most hospitals and clinics in the affected area and killed many health workers. According to World Health Organization (WHO) data, about half the deaths each year in Haiti are caused by HIV/AIDS, diseases causing severe diarrhea (including cholera and typhoid), respiratory infections, and meningitis. For the most part, these often-fatal illnesses can be prevented. Prevention would involve changes in lifestyle for some citizens and drastic improvements in sanitation facilities for most. Contaminated water is a major contributor to disease in Haiti. WHO estimates that 90 percent of Haiti's youngsters suffer from intestinal parasites and various diseases transmitted by polluted water. Thousands of Haitians also suffer from debilitating and often-fatal tuberculosis and malaria.

Bettering health conditions within an entire country involves many improvements, all of which are extremely costly. Physicians and other health-care workers must be trained (and once educated, encouraged to remain in the country). Hospitals and clinics must be built. Adequate funds must be made available to stock the supplies needed in health-related facilities. All citizens must have access to a clean and reliable supply of water and adequate sanitation facilities. Diets must be improved to include adequate vitamins, minerals, and protein. People must be educated in such basic hygienic matters as cleanliness. Something as simple as the use of soap and regular washing of hands would make a huge difference in people's health. Basically, Haitians must be better educated so they can make wiser choices and practice better hygiene.

FOODWAYS

Like most Caribbean islands, Haiti has a very rich and varied cuisine. Its culinary styles are a blend of many traditions, including Amerindian, various African cuisines, and French. Following the arrival of Europeans, ingredients from many areas of the world became available. Much of the Haitian diet is quite similar to that consumed throughout the Caribbean region. Common basic ingredients and strong African traditions have contributed to widespread similarities in foods and their preparation.

Most Haitians like their food hot and spicy (from peppers). Beans (of various types) and rice comes as close as any food to being a national dish. Beans, rice, and cornmeal are food staples. Remember the Creole pigs? Pork was a basic meat prior to the early 1980s when most of the country's pigs were killed following an outbreak of African swine fever virus. Fish, particularly red snapper, and other seafood, are dietary mainstays. Tomato, cabbage, avocado, okra, various types of peppers (mild and hot), and plantains (a banana-like fruit that is served cooked) are commonly used in preparing dishes.

The Haitian wealthy elite enjoy a diet much like that of affluent people anywhere. The popular French cuisine, of course, is world famous for its quality. But fine dining is expensive, and far beyond the reach of most Haitians.

FINE ARTS

Like the country's cuisine, Haitian fine arts offer a rich blend of French, African, and native Amerindian elements. Haitian artists are world-renowned for their distinctive painting and sculpture. Paintings are often a mix of bright colors depicting landscapes, markets, food, animals, dances, and various Voodoo rituals.

The earthquake took a terrible toll on Haiti's artistic community and legacy. Several artists and art-gallery owners died in the quake, as did the director of a major arts foundation. Additionally, several thousand art treasures worth tens of millions of dollars were lost, as were many of the galleries, museums, collectors' homes, churches, and government buildings in which paintings and sculptures were displayed or stored.

Haiti's music is a blend of African and European cultural influences. Early French colonial contributions are evident; so are significant Spanish styles borrowed from neighboring Dominican Republic and Cuba. From West Africa came several musical traditions. Over the years, they have combined to create

Art is displayed on the streets of Port-au-Prince. Haiti has a rich cultural history. Sadly, many important works of art were lost in the 2010 earthquake.

various styles that are unique to Haiti. These include Voodoo ceremonial traditions, ballads, parade music (*rara*), and the very popular *compas* (or *kompa* in Creole), which combines African rhythms and European-style dancing. It is played with a basic rhythm of *méringue* (from the Dominican Republic) and *tipico* (popular Panamanian folk music).

The best-known contemporary Haitian musical artist is Wyclef Jean. Jean moved to the United States in the late 1970s, when he was nine years old. His musical style can best be described as international. In addition to his favored hip-hop, at various times Jean has sung reggae, compas, rhythm and blues, folk, and *bachata*. The musical artist is also very active in promoting his native homeland. In January 2007 he became a roving ambassador to help improve Haiti's image abroad. Through a foundation that he created, thousands of Haitian youngsters have received scholarships to attend school. In 2010 he filed as a candidate for the country's presidency. However, he was ruled ineligible because he had not lived in Haiti for the past five years.

SPORTS

Football (soccer) is the most popular competitive sport in Haiti. There are several hundred small football clubs scattered about the country, and most compete at the local level. Haiti's national team has been largely unsuccessful in international competition. At least 30 Haitian Soccer Federation members died during the earthquake.

Basketball is growing in popularity. Haiti has had two native-born players in the National Basketball Association (NBA). Samuel Dalembert (now a Canadian citizen) began playing with the Philadelphia 76ers in 2001, and Olden Polynice played with various NBA teams over a long and successful career.

Perhaps the greatest surprise relating to sports in Haiti is one in which they *do not* excel and seemingly have little interest—baseball. Haiti and neighboring Dominican Republic both have about the same population, between 9 and 10 million. Amazingly, more than 500 athletes from the Dominican Republic have played or currently play major-league baseball in the United States. In fact, one of every seven of today's major league players is from the "DR," yet not a single Haitian has ever played for a U.S. major league team.

LOOKING AHEAD

Basic elements of culture—language, religion, diet, social interactions, and so forth—are not changed by natural disasters such as hurricanes or earthquakes. The lives of people, however, are often changed, and changed drastically, by such events. Much of this chapter has painted a dismal picture of life in Haiti today. Will it improve soon?

8

Haiti
Looks Ahead

Throughout this geographic study of Haiti, three very important themes have been followed. First, we have been concerned with "What is where, why there, and why care?" in regard to various elements and conditions within the country. Take, for example, the country's frequent natural disasters. Earthquakes can be explained by "where." Haiti lies astride two major fault lines, the edges of active tectonic plates. The severe tropical storms that frequently rake the country are also easily explained by "where." The country is located squarely in the middle of the North Atlantic hurricane track. Therefore, it can be predicted with certainty that the country will continue to be ravaged by occasional seismic tremors and tropical storms.

A second theme has been Erhard Rostlund's belief that "the present is the fruit of the past and contains the seeds of the future." By now, it is likely that you understand and appreciate the importance of historical events in molding Haiti's current conditions. French colonial status is still imprinted on its language, religion, and several other aspects of culture. People (including race and ethnicity), much of the diet, the Creole tongue, Voodoo, and many other traits owe their presence to the ancestral African origin of most Haitians. Throughout much of the book, you have been made aware of the very close relationship between government, economics, and other conditions. From the very outset of independence in 1804, Haiti has been very poorly governed throughout most of its history.

Finally, there is the wisdom of the old Creole saying *Deye mon, gen mon*, or "Beyond the mountains, more mountains." For most Haitians, life has been a constant struggle. Both natural forces and human shortcomings have repeatedly put up barriers that hinder progress. If nothing more, the Haitian people must be admired for their courage and stamina in the face of huge and seemingly insurmountable obstacles.

WHAT MUST BE DONE?

If Haiti is to progress, many things must be done. Whether the country can succeed in the various tasks is anyone's guess. Here, the author's "crystal ball" becomes incredibly murky!

First and foremost, it is essential that the country's political system become honest, stable, and responsive to the people. The near-universal tradition of corruption must be stopped. It is disgraceful that Haiti ranks very near the bottom among the countries rated in the Corruption Perception Index. It is not Haiti's common people who are at fault for this deplorable ranking; rather, it is the irresponsibility of so many people in positions of leadership.

If the foregoing can be achieved, the country's economy will improve. Haitians themselves, let alone foreigners, are reluctant to invest in a poorly governed and corrupt country. If the economy improves, most all the other problems will begin to fade away. Needed infrastructure can be built if funds are available. Education can be improved, as can health care. If jobs are available, an essential middle class can be developed. This will narrow the yawning and socially dangerous gap between the country's very wealthy and extremely poor classes.

Haiti lacks significant natural resources, and its population remains poorly educated. Before a white-collar, service-based economy can develop, many more of the country's people must become trained. Currently, about 80 percent of the country's college graduates leave Haiti to work elsewhere. This brain drain represents a tremendous loss of potential human resources needed to spur economic development. With an improved government and economy, many more well-educated Haitians will remain in their country and contribute to its future prosperity.

As is true in many less-developed countries, tourism offers excellent potential for development. Most tourism-related jobs do not require extensive training of a workforce. Capital resources can be used to develop a tourism-based infrastructure in selected locations (Mexico's development of Cancun as a tourist destination is an excellent example) to include lodging, restaurants, adequate transportation routes and means such as buses and rental cars, and other facilities. There also must be things for visitors to see and do. Haiti offers many interesting sights that range from its vibrant people and their culture to the sun, surf, and sand of its many tropical beaches.

Those concerned with environmental issues certainly will be interested in Haiti's ravaged landscape and how it might be restored. Here and there are remnants of tropical rain forest that can be developed as ecotourism destinations. The country's rugged terrain offers many spectacular views and a variety of interesting ecosystems.

Tourists interested in history and architecture might be attracted to a number of structures, including the massive Citadelle Laferrière (the Citadel). This magnificent mountain-top structure is a UNESCO World Heritage Site. It was built by Henri Christophe, a leader of the Haitian slave rebellion following the country's independence from France. The gigantic stone structure is the largest building in the Americas that was constructed as a fortress. Twenty thousand laborers worked on the Citadel for 15 years, completing the task in 1820. The fortress was intended to protect newly independent Haiti from French attack. It was outfitted with 365 cannons and huge stockpiles of cannonballs, both of which remain at the site today. The structure is a short distance from Cap Haitien, which is already developed as a tourist destination.

POST-EARTHQUAKE HAITI

Perhaps the largest question pertaining to Haiti's future is how the country will rebound from the January 12, 2010, earthquake. A year after the tragic event, there was little room for optimism. According to most news releases, the Haitian government has been largely slow and inadequate in its response to the tragedy. More than one million people remain in squalid refugee camps. They have no money and no places of their own to go. The government has attempted to find suitable land on which to rebuild but has been largely unsuccessful. Most Haitians, you must remember, are squatters who live on land they do not own.

Should Port-au-Prince be rebuilt on its present site? One thing is certain: The fault it sits on will slip again and again. The only question is when. Should the city be rebuilt elsewhere on safer ground? There are many problems facing those who will finally make the decision. For example, in Port-au-Prince most property was owned, whereas at a new site, one can only question how ownership would be determined. (Historically, many cities destroyed by some natural catastrophe have been rebuilt in the same hazard-prone location. For example, Lisbon, Portugal, and San Francisco, California, were rebuilt on-site following devastating earthquakes.)

An aerial view of Citadelle Laferrière, which was built for protection after Haiti gained independence from France. Sites such as this can attract tourists, which could help Haiti's economy considerably.

Nearly $10 billion in foreign aid was promised by various countries, agencies, and other donors following the quake. Very little of it, however, has been received. Some "official" estimates now suggest that the country will be fortunate to receive 15–20 percent of the promised aid. This, of course, is very disturbing. Are people and countries becoming less generous? The answer is no—but they do want accountability and some assurance that their gifts will not vanish into the very deep pocket of some political opportunist. In today's Haiti, they have no such guarantee.

Just when many things were beginning to appear more favorable in terms of Haiti's future, catastrophe struck. No other country has ever experienced a more devastating natural disaster. Its toll in human and economic losses, as a percentage of a country's population and GDP, is the greatest ever. It will take Haiti and so many of its people decades to recover, and many of the losses can never be recovered.

For Haitians, will the day ever come when they no longer face a seemingly endless series of mountains beyond mountains? Will they one day reach a mountain crest and see spread out below them a broad and fertile plain that stretches to the distant horizon? Let us hope that such a time will come, and soon.

General Information

Country Name

Conventional long form	Republic of Haiti
Conventional short form	Haiti
Local long form	Republique d'Haiti/Ayiti
Local short form	Haiti/Ayiti
Location	North America; between Caribbean Sea and North Atlantic Ocean; occupies western one-third of Hispaniola (island shared with the Dominican Republic)
Capital	Port-au-Prince (established 1749; became capital in 1804; primate city with metropolitan population of estimated 3 million; devastated by severe earthquake in 2010)
Territory	10,714 square miles (27,749 square kilometers); slightly larger than Massachusetts
Boundaries	224 miles (360 kilometers) with Dominican Republic; 1,100-mile (1,770-km) coastline facing Atlantic Ocean and Caribbean Sea

Physical Geography

Land	Mostly rugged and mountainous, with narrow river valleys and coastal plains; highest point, Chaine de la Selle, 8,793 feet (2,680 meters)
Climate	Wet-dry tropical, with little seasonal variation in temperature; sharp seasonal patterns of precipitation, with high-sun period wet and low-sun period dry; northeast trade winds throughout the year
Natural resources	Bauxite, copper, calcium carbonate, gold, marble, hydropower
Land use	Land suited to agriculture: 28%; land permanently farmed: 12%; other: 60% (2005)
Irrigated land	355 square miles (919 sq. km) (2003)
Natural hazards	Earthquakes; frequent hurricanes from June through October; floods, droughts, landslides
Environmental issues	Severe deforestation, soil erosion, inadequate supply of good water in heavily populated areas, water pollution

Facts at a Glance

Population Geography

	(July 2010 estimates unless otherwise indicated)
Population	9,035,536 (last census 2006; current estimates vary from 8.9 million to 9.7 million)
Population density	840 per square mile (323 per sq. km)
Settlement	53% rural, 47% urban (2008 estimate); with Port-au-Prince and neighboring communities in ruins, many people are housed in rural camps
Age structure	0–14 years: 38.1%
	15–64 years: 58.5%
	65 years and over: 3.4%
Median age	Total population: 21.1 years (male: 20.9 years; female: 21.4 years)
Population growth rate	1.84% to 2.1% per year (depending upon source)
Birthrate	31 births/1,000 population
Death rate	10 deaths/1,000 population
Infant mortality rate	60 deaths/1,000 live births
Migration rate	-2.07 migrant(s)/1,000 population (out-migration has increased dramatically since the January 2010 earthquake)
Life expectancy at birth	Total population: 60.8 years (male: 59.1 years; female: 62.5 years)
Total fertility rate	3.81 (average number of children given birth per woman during her lifetime; 2.1 is replacement rate)
HIV/AIDS prevalence	2.2% of population; 7,200 deaths annually (2007 est.)

Human Geography

Nationality	Haitian
Racial/ethnic groups	Black (95%), mulatto (black and white mix) 4%, white less than 1%
Official languages	French and Creole
Religions	Roman Catholic 80%, Protestant 16% (Baptist 10%, Pentecostal 4%, Adventist 1%, other 1%), other 3%, none 1%; roughly half of the population practices Voodoo, which has been elevated to status of an official religion
Literacy	Total population over age 15 able to read and write: 53% (male: 54.8%; female: 51.5%) (2003 est.)
Education expenditures	1.5% of GDP (estimate)

Human Development Index 145 among the world's 169 ranked countries (lowest in the Americas)

Government

Government	Republic
Administrative divisions	10 departments: Artibonite, Centre, Grand'Anse, Nippes, Nord, Nord-Est, Nord-Ouest, Ouest, Sud, Sud-Est
Independence	January 1, 1804 (from France); world's first black republic; second oldest independent country in the Americas
Current constitution	March 10, 1987; suspended on several occasions and reinstated in 2006
Branches of government	Executive: President is chief of state; prime minister is head of government; president elected to five-year term and may not serve consecutive terms; prime minister appointed by president, ratified by the National Assembly
Legislative	Bicameral National Assembly consists of Senate (30 seats; members elected to six-year terms by popular vote, with one-third elected every two years) and Chamber of Deputies (99 seats; members elected to four-year terms by popular vote)
Judicial	Supreme Court
Political parties	27 (12 major, 15 other)

Economy

	(2009 estimates; most data are for conditions preearthquake)
Gross domestic product	Figures range between $7.0 and $11.99 billion
Rate of economic growth	2.9%
Per capita GDP-PPP	Figures range between $790 and $1,300 (lowest in Western Hemisphere)
GDP by sector	Agriculture 28%; industry 20%; services 52% (2004 est.)
Employment by sector	Agriculture 66%; industry 9%; services 25% (1995 est.)
Unemployment	No data available (est. two-thirds of population unemployed or underemployed; much higher after 2010 earthquake)
Population below poverty line	80%
Agriculture	Coffee, mangoes, sugarcane, rice, corn, sorghum, wood

Facts at a Glance

Industry   Sugar refining, flour milling, textiles, cement, light assembly based on imported parts

Exports $559 million: apparel, manufactures, oils, cocoa, mangoes, coffee

Export partners   United States 80%, Dominican Republic 7%, Canada 3%, others 10%

Imports $2.05 billion ($1.49 billion trade deficit); food, manufactured goods, machinery and transport equipment, fuels, raw materials

Import partners   United States 33%, Dominican Republic 24%, Netherlands Antilles 11%, China 5%, others 27%

Transportation   *Roadways*: 2,585 miles (4,160 km), of which 628 miles (1,011 km) are paved; *Airports*: 14 (4 with paved runways); *Railway*: none; *Seaports:* Port-au-Prince and Saint-Marc

Communications

Infrastructure   (Communications received widespread damage as a result of the earthquake; data appearing below are pre-earthquake conditions.)

Telephones   About 110,000 mainline telephones and 3.2 million cellular phones

Radio broadcast stations   67 (41 AM, 26 FM)

Television broadcast stations   2 plus cable service

Internet users   estimated 1 million users

*source: CIA-*The World Factbook* (2010)

1492   Christopher Columbus lands on the north coast near present-day Cap Haitien and claims the island of Hispaniola for Spain.

1503   The first Africans arrive on Hispaniola as laborers.

1508   Spaniards officially establish the African slave trade.

1528   The first Roman Catholic bishop is appointed to Hispaniola.

1625   The French settle Tortuga Island and the northwestern coast of Hispaniola and name their colony Saint Domingue.

1665   The French establish a settlement at Port-de-Paix on Haiti's north coast.

1670   France authorizes African slave trade in Saint Domingue.

1697   Spain signs the Treaty of Ryswick, which cedes the western third of Hispaniola to France.

1749   Port-au-Prince is founded and named capital of Saint Domingue.

1752   Slave rebellions begin in northern Saint Domingue; they continue throughout the remainder of the century.

1790s   The decade sees widespread slave rebellions and resulting armed conflicts involving Africans against Spanish and French forces.

1793   Slavery is abolished in northern Saint Domingue, but without French consent.

1794   The French National Convention declares the abolition of slavery in all French colonies.

1801   Toussaint Louverture invades eastern Hispaniola and captures the city of Santo Domingo. He declares freedom for all slaves and appoints a 10-member Central Assembly to issue a constitution; a constitution is drafted appointing Toussaint as governor-general-for-life.

1802	The French invade and capture local forces; Toussaint surrenders.
1803	Toussaint dies in a French prison. In the last major battle of the revolution, forces led by Jean-Jacques Dessalines and Alexandre Pétion defeat the French.
1804	On January 1, Dessalines declares Haiti's independence from France and himself as emperor of the new republic. Port-au-Prince becomes the capital.
1806	Dessalines is assassinated.
1822	Jean-Pierre Boyer, president-for-life of the Republic of Haiti, claims control of the entire island of Hispaniola.
1842	A severe earthquake strikes northern Haiti, destroying the city of Cap Haitien.
1844	The Dominican Republic declares its independence from Haiti.
1862	The United States recognizes Haiti.
1912	The Haitian American Sugar Company is established.
1915	Three thousand U.S. Marines enter Port-au-Prince, beginning a 19-year U.S. occupation of Haiti.
1929	Haiti and the Dominican Republic sign an agreement establishing the present-day boundary between the two nations.
1933	The United States agrees to end its occupation of Haiti; the last forces leave the following year.
1937	Between 17,000 and 35,000 Haitians living in the Dominican Republic are massacred by military forces.
1957	Dr. François "Papa Doc" Duvalier is elected president of Haiti.
1964	After a reign of terror against his enemies, Duvalier becomes president-for-life.
1970s	Thousands of Haitians flee the country, many by boat to Florida.
1971	President-for-life Duvalier dies and is succeeded by his son, Jean-Claude "Baby Doc" Duvalier, as president-for-life.

1986 Under pressure of rising dissent against his leadership, President Jean-Claude Duvalier flees Haiti and establishes exile in France.

1987 A new constitution is adopted.

1994 The United States, with UN sanction, sends troops to occupy Haiti.

2000 The last UN peacekeeping forces leave Haiti.

2003 Voodoo is recognized as a religion, with rights equal to other faiths.

2004 An uprising against Jean-Bertrand Aristide forces the president into exile; UN peacekeeping troops reenter Haiti; Hurricane Jeanne kills an estimated 3,000 in northern Haiti.

2006 In a general election, René Préval is declared winner of the presidential vote; a democratically elected government takes office.

2008 Prime Minister Alexis is dismissed by Parliament; widespread food riots occur; Hurricane Hanna and other storms leave nearly eight hundred dead.

2009 Former U.S. president Bill Clinton is appointed UN special representative to Haiti; the World Bank and the International Monetary Fund cancel 80 percent of Haiti's debt.

2010 A major earthquake measuring 7.0 on the Richter scale kills an estimated 230,000, injures an estimated 300,000 more, and destroys much of Port-au-Prince and surrounding communities. Anger grows over the slow and inadequate government response to the tragedy.

Bibliography

Brubaker, Bill. "The Art of Resilience." *Smithsonian* (May 2010): 36–48.

———. "Frustration Sets In." *The Economist* (July 31, 2010), 26–27.

CIA. The World Fact Book (2010). http://www.cia.gov/library/publications/the-world-factbook/geos/ha.html

Corruption Perception Index. http://www.transparency.org/policy_research/surveys_indices/cpi

Heinl, Robert. *Written in Blood: The History of the Haitian People.* Lantham, Md.: University Press of America, 1996.

Human Development Index. http://hdr.undp.org/en/statistics/

James, C.L.R. *The Black Jacobins.* New York: Vintage Books, 1990.

Masters, Jeffrey. "Hurricanes and Haiti: A Tragic History." http://www.wunderground.com/education/haiti.asp

Revol, Didier. "Hoping for change in Haiti's Cité-Soleil." (2006). International Red Cross. http://www.redcross.int/EN/mag/magazine2006_2/10-11.html.

West, Robert Cooper, and John P. Augelli. *Middle America: Its Lands and Peoples.* Englewood, N.J.: Prentice-Hall, 1966/1989.

Books

Abbott, Elizabeth. *Haiti: The Duvaliers and Their Legacy.* New York: McGraw-Hill, 1988.

Arthur, Charles. *Haiti in Focus: A Guide to the People, Politics, and Culture.* New York: Interlink Books, 2002.

Clammer, Paul, Michael Grosberg, and Jens Porup. *Dominican Republic & Haiti.* Victoria, Australia: Lonely Planet Publications, 2008.

Dash, J. Michael. *Culture and Customs of Haiti.* Westport, Conn.: Greenwood Press, 2001.

Dupuy, Alex. *Haiti in the World Economy: Class, Race, and Underdevelopment since 1700.* Boulder, Colo.: Westview Press, 1989.

Girard, Philippe. *Haiti: The Tumultuous History—From Pearl of the Caribbean to Broken Nation.* New York: Palgrave Macmillan, 2005.

Gold, Herbert. *Haiti: Best Nightmare on Earth.* Piscataway, N.J.: Transaction Publishers, 2001.

Gritzner, Charles F., and D.A. Phillips. *The Dominican Republic.* New York: Chelsea House, 2010.

Heinl, Robert Debs, and Nancy Gordon Heinl. *Written in Blood: The Story of the Haitian People, 1492–1995.* Lanham, Md.: University Press of America, 1996/2005.

Kidder, Tracy. *Mountains Beyond Mountains: Healing the World.* New York: Random House Trade Paperbacks, 2009.

McAlister, Elizabeth A. *Rara! Vodou, Power, and Performance in Haiti and Its Diaspora.* Berkeley and Los Angeles: University of California Press, 2003.

Metreaux, Alfred. *Haiti.* New York: Schocken/Random House, 1989.

Web Sites

BBC News–Timeline: Haiti
http://news.bbc.co.uk/2/hi/americas/1202857.stm

CIA–The World Factbook (Haiti)
https://www.cia.gov/library/publications/the-world-factbook/geos/ha.html
Primary source of statistical data

Embassy of Haiti in the United States
http://www.haiti.org/

Further Reading

Infoplease: Haiti
http://www.infoplease.com/ipa/A0107612.html?pageno=2

Lonely Planet (Travel Guide): Haiti
http://www.lonelyplanet.com/haiti

ReliefWeb
http://www.reliefweb.int/rw/dbc.nsf/doc100?OpenForm
Excellent source of information for current environmental
  disasters

NationMaster
http://www.nationmaster.com/index.php
Provides country rankings in numerous categories

U.S. Department of State, Background Note: Haiti
http://www.state.gov/r/pa/ei/bgn/1982.htm

Wikipedia: Wyclef Jean
http://en.wikipedia.org/wiki/Wyclef_Jean
Biographical information on Wyclef Jean and his brilliant musical career

Picture Credits

Index

Index

CHARLES F. "FRITZ" GRITZNER is Distinguished Professor Emeritus of Geography at South Dakota State University in Brookings. In 2010 he retired after a 50-year career of college teaching. In retirement, Dr. Gritzner; his wife, Yvonne; and their "family" of two Italian greyhounds remain in South Dakota. He enjoy enjoys travel, writing, and sharing his love for and knowledge of geography with readers. As a senior consulting editor and author for Chelsea House Publishers' MODERN WORLD NATIONS, MAJOR WORLD CULTURES, EXTREME ENVIRONMENTS, and GLOBAL CONNECTIONS series, Fritz has a wonderful opportunity to combine each of these "hobbies." He has served as both president and executive director of the National Council for Geographic Education (NCGE) and has received the council's highest honor, the George J. Miller Award for Distinguished Service to Geographic Education, as well as numerous other national teaching, service, and research recognitions from the NCGE, the Association of American Geographers, and other organizations.